THE AUTHOR

Dr Mahmoud Ayoub teaches in the Department of Religion, Temple University, Philadelphia, U.S.A. Born in Southern Lebanon, he received his BA in Philosophy from the American University, Beirut, his MA in Religious Thought from the University of Pennsylvania and his PhD in Comparative Religion from Harvard University. He is the author of several publications and has been particularly active in the area of Muslim-Christian dialogue including lecturing on the subject in the Philippines, Lebanon, England and the Vatican.

Islam and the Third Universal Theory: The Religious Thought of Mu'ammar al-Qadhdhafi

Mahmoud Ayoub

KEGAN PAUL INTERNATIONAL
London and New York

First published in 1987 by
Kegan Paul International Ltd
PO Box 256, London WC1B 3SW, England

First paperback edition published 1991

Distributed by
John Wiley & Sons Ltd
Southern Cross Trading Estate
1 Oldlands Way, Bognor Regis
West Sussex, PO22 9SA, England

Routledge, Chapman & Hall Inc
29 West 35th Street
New York, NY 10001, USA

The Canterbury Press Pty Ltd
Unit 2, 71 Rushdale Street
Scoresby, Victoria 3179, Australia

© Mahmoud Mustafa Ayoub 1987

Printed in Great Britain by T.J. Press (Padstow) Ltd.

British Library Cataloguing in Publication Data
Ayoub, Mahmoud M. (Mahmoud Mustafa)
 Islam and third Universal theory.
 1. Islam. Theories of al – Quadhdh af i, Mu ammar
 I. Title
 297.092

ISBN 0-7103-0404-8

US Library of Congress Cataloging-in-Publication Data
Applied for

Contents

Preface

One of the most controversial figures of modern times has been Colonel Mu'ammar al-Qadhdhafi, leader of the Libyan popular revolution of 1 September 1969 and author of the 'Third Universal Theory'. For the West, and especially the Western media, Qadhdhafi is the villain of the piece, master terrorist and close ally of communist Russia. For conservative Arab rulers, Qadhdhafi is 'the madman of Libya', and an atheist communist. For millions of the oppressed of Asia, Africa and Latin America, Qadhdhafi is a hero, a comrade in the revolutionary struggle against imperialism, exploitation and racism. In short, al-Qadhdhafi has been loved and hated, admired and ridiculed, and above all feared as an impulsive politician who refuses to play the usual games of international diplomacy.

The personality and intellectual makeup of Mu'ammar al-Qadhdhafi were formed in the desert, where austerity and simplicity of life provide the basic framework within which he was born and nurtured. Thus his insistence on a simple and straightforward approach to Islam as a religious faith and system of values is an integral part of his desert character. It is, moreover, this uncompromising character which has earned him the condemnation of many traditional Muslim religious leaders and movements, and provided his opponents among Arab rulers with a powerful weapon to use against him in their propaganda, in both the East and West. It is the religious dimension of Qadhdhafi's thought which has been least studied, but which deserves close attention because it provides the foundation and framework of his ideology and public life in all its aspects.

The aim of this work is to present an objective and comprehensive study of Mu'ammar al-Qadhdhafi's religious thinking and its place in his political, economic and social philosophy. My task is not to judge Qadhdhafi as a leader, his sincerity as a man of faith, or to determine the degree of success in implementing his philosophy at home or abroad. It is rather to present to Muslim and non-Muslim readers a true picture of his religious thought and convictions as a Muslim. This I shall attempt in the hope that unfounded speculations about Qadhdhafi's thought and personality will, at least, be questioned as a major source of information. I can do no better in fulfilling this purpose than to let Qadhdhafi speak for himself.

I have relied in my research for this study on a variety of primary and secondary sources. The most important source is, of course, Qadhdhafi's own words. These have been preserved in annual volumes collectively entitled *al-Sijill al-Qawmi* (The National Record). These important volumes provide, in chronological order from the start of the revolution, 1 September 1969, to the present, all the speeches, media interviews, press conferences and public addresses which Qadhdhafi has delivered on both religious and national occasions. His religious addresses and discourses have also been collected in a volume entitled *Khutab wa-Ahadith al-Qa'id al-Diniyah*, which constitutes an important primary source for this discussion. *The Green Book* and commentaries on it written by Qadhdhafi himself and others provide the primary source for our understanding of the type of society which he envisages for his country and the rest of humankind.

The works of Libyan thinkers produced by the International Institute for Studies and Research on *The Green Book*, in books, pamphlets and monographs, are especially significant because they reflect the views, analyses and judgements of the people most directly concerned with the Third Universal Theory and its application in real life. Mu'ammar al-Qadhdhafi is a devoted Arab nationalist. His words and ideas are addressed first and foremost to the Arab people of his country and the rest of the Arab world. Thus, Arab writers who have dealt with his ideological and political thought must be given serious attention as important, albeit secondary, sources. The works of Western writers – journalists, political scientists and historians – are used only as sources for our understanding of Western attitudes towards Colonel Qadhdhafi and his thought.

The biographical portrait of Qadhdhafi, so sensitively and sympathetically presented by Mirella Bianco, will be used as an important primary source in discussing Qadhdhafi's formative years before the revolution. The book appeared first in French under the title *Kadhafi, Messager du Desert*, and was subsequently translated into English under the title *Gadafi, Voice from the Desert*. It is generally regarded as the chief biography of Qadhdhafi, even by the Libyan authorities, who had the book translated into Arabic. The author based her work on first-hand information gathered through extensive travel in Libya and elsewhere, interviewing a large number of people who knew or worked with Qadhdhafi, including his parents and other members of his family and tribe.

While the present study will deal mainly with Mu'ammar al-Qadhdhafi's religious thought, it will none the less attempt to do so in the context of his general philosophy known as the Third Universal Theory, and contained chiefly in *The Green Book*. It is important, therefore, to present first the man and his intellectual development from his childhood to the start of the revolution, when the major aspects of this theory and its application reached their fruition. This will be the concern of the first chapter of this book. In this chapter, we shall look at Qadhdhafi through the eyes of those who have admired him and have remained his loyal supporters. These somewhat laudative impressions are in fact our only source of information about Qadhdhafi before the revolution. In the second part of this chapter we shall follow the first steps of the revolution from its inception to its execution.

The second chapter will discuss Qadhdhafi's vision of the 'new society of the masses' as presented in *The Green Book*. This chapter will consist of three parts, dealing with the political, economic and social structures respectively.

The third chapter will deal with Qadhdhafi's faith as a Muslim thinker. It will be divided into four parts. The first will deal with Qadhdhafi's view of Islam as a universal religion, and its relationship with other faiths, notably Judaism and Christianity. The second will present his view of the Qur'an and Prophetic Tradition as sources of the law of society. The third part will examine the relation of Islam to politics in contemporary society. Qadhdhafi's vision of a just society is based on his theory of the 'new Islamic socialism', which will be discussed in the final section of this chapter.

In *The Green Book* Qadhdhafi argues that religion and nationalism are the two primary forces moving human history. The fourth chapter of this study will deal with this assertion. It will examine the role of religion and nationalism in the process of human history, the role and mission of the Arab nation, and the predicament of national minorities in the larger national and religious societies of the modern world.

The concluding chapter of this work will briefly examine Mu'ammar al-Qadhdhafi's image in the West, and as projected by some Arab rulers. My aim in this chapter is not to be exhaustive, as I believe this will serve no good purpose, but rather to contrast this image with the man as he appears through his own self-presentation.

Several years ago I suggested to the general secretary of the Islamic Call Society the need for a book that would concentrate on Colonel Qadhdhafi's religious, and especially Islamic, ideas, convictions and commitments. The idea was accepted, and I was asked to undertake this task. I am grateful to the Society for encouraging this project both morally and materially. I wish also to express my appreciation to the people of Libya for their friendliness and hospitality. They too share in that refreshing simplicity and genuineness so characteristic of a desert people. It is to them that I present this modest contribution, which I trust will help in a small way in promoting better understanding and cooperation among people of different faiths and ideologies.

I shall attempt in this work to present a non-apologetic but positive picture of Qadhdhafi, the man and his thought. Most of the literature dealing with Colonel Qadhdhafi has been apologetic both in its praise and condemnation. While striving to avoid these pitfalls, I lay no claim to perfection. My work will have its shortcomings, for which I alone am responsible.

M. M. Ayoub
December 1985

1
Qadhdhafi's Dream

Qadhdhafi's Background and Youth

'The Bedouins have no walls and gates. Therefore, they provide their own defense and do not entrust it to or rely upon others for it. They watch carefully all sides of the road. . . . They go into the desert, guided by their fortitude, putting their trust in themselves. Fortitude has become a character quality of theirs, and courage their nature.'[1]

The old civilizations of Egypt and Mesopotamia were born on the banks of the Nile and the two rivers. They were, however, close to the desert by which they were nurtured and refined. It was in the desert that God spoke to Moses, and the children of Israel were disciplined and purified. In the desert the ancient revolutionary prophet Elijah heard the 'still voice of God' ordering him to face the tyranny of an oppressive king.[2] In the desert, Christ prepared himself through fasting and prayers for a mission which was to shape Western history. In the solitude of the desert the prophet Muhammad contemplated the order of creation and the sad state of his own people.

In the desert heaven and earth meet. The vast expanse of sand mirrors the Absolute in its stillness and raging fury. The desert is the epitome of simplicity and calm, eternal sameness and precarious change, austerity and freedom.

The people of the desert live with and like the sandy expanse of their habitat. They are always on the move in search of water and herbage for themselves and their animals, and dream of 'gardens beneath which rivers flow'.[3] Thus their character is formed by the desert – by the frugality that comes from the uncertainties of life, by

11

the hospitality which is dictated by the will to share the basic amenities of life, and by the will to raid and plunder dictated by the ever-present spectres of hunger and thirst. The desert is the home both of oases and of an aridity, caused by long drought or the sudden downpour of torrential rain – rain 'with which God revives the earth after its death'.[4]

These are the qualities of the desert which become the qualities of the austere, free and uncompromising character of its men and women. In the desert Mu'ammar al-Qadhdhafi was born, lived, dreamed and reflected. From an early age he appeared to be different from other children. He was serious, even taciturn; yet his stern countenance was always tempered with an inquisitive smile. He was an only son to a family who lived in the desert, far from the city and its demands and benefits. Mu'ammar seldom played with his cousins; rather he was always lost in thought about one thing or another.[5]

Mu'ammar's father was a poor man living in a tent in the Sirte Desert. In the same tent, in which Mu'ammar's parents continued to live even after the revolution had secured homes for most city dwellers, he was born. To this day he returns often to his desert birthplace to resume his life in a tent among the members of his tribe and family. His father recalled these visits, saying, 'Yes, he often comes. He sleeps on his old mat. He takes up the old way of living, and you simply cannot imagine how he thrives here in the desert.'[6]

Although himself an illiterate man, Mu'ammar's father was anxious that his only son receive some education. He therefore brought a teacher of the Qur'an from the city to teach his seven-year-old son and his cousins to read the Qur'an. Mu'ammar never left his teacher and showed an extraordinary desire for learning. At the age of nine or ten, Mu'ammar was sent to the Sirte elementary school, about 30 kilometres away from his home. As his father could afford no lodging for his son, Mu'ammar slept in the mosque. Every Thursday the youth returned home on foot to spend Friday with his parents and walk back to school that evening. Mu'ammar took full advantage of the opportunity for formal education, completing six years of elementary schooling in four years.

Four years later, when Mu'ammar was fourteen years old, the Qadhdhafi family moved to Sabha, the main town of the Fezzan district. The purpose of this move was to give the young boy a chance to pursue his secondary education. While yet a child, Mu'ammar loved to listen to stories of the bitter struggle of his people against their colonizers. He would have his father tell him for the hundredth time the story of how Mu'ammar's grandfather fell in battle against the Italian colonialists, and how he himself was wounded in his left shoulder in the same struggle after the First World War. Every time he heard the story he would again ask his father, 'And who was your leader?'

'A Turk,' his father would reply patiently, as he repeated the story many times over.[7] This proud shepherd boy saw the only cause of his people's sufferings to be the foreigners. He often fell asleep as he dreamed of new adventures, of new struggles against new colonialists, of revolution and of a new kind of liberty. Mu'ammar's youth coincided with the successful Egyptian revolution of 1952, and the Algerian struggle against French colonialism. Thus it was in Sirte that his political ideas began to take shape.

Even as a youth, Mu'ammar al-Qadhdhafi was admired by his fellow students at the Sabha secondary school for his passionate interest in politics and his ability to stir students to action by his impassioned speeches. He used any political issue or significant event as a good occasion for a demonstration: the Algerian revolution, French testing of an atom bomb over the Sahara, the death of Patrice Lumumba and the dissolution of the Syrian-Egyptian union in 1961 were only a few examples. During his third year at Sabha, the school authorities expelled him because he was considered a dangerous political agitator. In Sabha, Mu'ammar formed a small circle of like-minded friends to whom he confided his political ideas. Among these were people like 'Abd al-Salam al-Jalloud and others who have remained close associates of Colonel Qadhdhafi throughout his political career.

In 1961 Qadhdhafi transferred to Misrata, a city near Tripoli, where two years later he completed his secondary education. It was in Misrata that he formed the first effective civilian political movement prior to the revolution. The movement included civil servants, teachers and other professionals from different parts of the country. This movement was to be free from any party identity or ideological preference. It was rather to be a purely Libyan movement in aim and character, but with Arab national unity as its ultimate goal. Arab unity has remained Qadhdhafi's lifelong dream and pre-occupation. To it, and it alone, he has devoted all his energies, as will be amply demonstrated throughout this study. In Misrata, Qadhdhafi realized that the only way to liberate his country from external exploitation and internal corruption was through a revolution that would overthrow the regime of King Idris and reorganize society on the principles of justice, equality and a fair distribution of wealth. He thus urged a number of close student friends to join the military, so as to form the nucleus of a corps of Unionist Free Officers. As the name of this important group of officers indicates, they were to be committed to Arab unity and liberty of the Libyan and all the Arab peoples. Qadhdhafi himself joined the military academy in Benghazi in 1963. There he formed the movement of the Unionist Free Officers in the following year. The character and aims of this movement are described in Colonel Qadhdhafi's memoirs. The first revolutionary movement began in the fifties in Sabha among the students. In 1964 a Central Committee composed exclusively of military personnel was formed. Another civilian committee was also formed, which was to be independent from the movement of the Unionist Free Officers, who made up the Central Committee.[8] An axiom of this movement was freedom from any party politics. It was to be characterized by flexibility and breadth. It was to avoid at all costs narrow cliquishness and sterile disputation. These characteristics helped protect the movement from being found out, and prevented the authorities from discovering its ultimate goals.[9]

It was observed at the start of this chapter that the desert forms and nurtures the character of its people. It may not be too presumptuous to add here that the desert is the right soil for single-mindedness, clarity of vision, and even the faith in the one and omnipotent divine sovereign. 'The voice of the wilderness' was that of Zarathustra, the ancient prophets of Israel, John the Baptist, Jesus of Nazareth and Muhammad, all calling humankind to a faith commitment to the One God. Their message was one in its uncompromising moral strictness and the demand of a holy life before the holy God. It is in this sense, as we shall see later, that Qadhdhafi insisted that they all preached the message of total submission (*islam*) to the will of God. Qadhdhafi shares this moral strictness and leaning towards a holy life, as have all the desert people throughout the centuries of Jewish, Christian and Islamic history.

Mme Bianco has with great discernment recognized these qualities in Mu'ammar al-Qadhdhafi's character. She says: 'It is in the desert that one may seek out the very essence of Qadhdhafi's nature, of the spirituality, of the mysticism which have greater weight than any of his aspirations, and which influence even his political action.' Still more concisely, Mme Bianco continues: 'It is precisely this concept of liberty, the intangible freedom of desert people – a freedom entirely one's own, and yet a submission to God, and God alone – which underlies all the choices, decisions and actions taken by Qadhdhafi; even, and perhaps essentially, those of a political nature.'[10]

Mme Bianco wrote these reflections after lengthy meetings with Mu'ammar's family, acquaintances and colleagues. In fact, her view of Qadhdhafi has been coloured by the words of his father and some of his closest associates. Since the aim of this discussion is not to present a biography of Qadhdhafi but, rather, a character sketch, I will present at some length the impressions of his father and of his close friends of his character. Mu'ammar was so serious and taciturn, his father observed, that one had to ask direct questions to make him speak. When asked about his son's basic characteristics, the old man answered, 'Courage and intelligence. His love of his family. His piety.'[11] This view is corroborated by many of those who were interviewed by Mme Bianco. Mu'ammar's old schoolteacher described him as a man of great intelligence, of sobriety bordering on asceticism, and a deep piety.[12] Qadhdhafi was a true son of the desert who feared no one but God. He was kind and helpful to friends, but severe when made angry. Muhammad Khalil, an old member of the civilian movement and friend of Qadhdhafi, describes the special qualities of his friend: 'They are his intelligence, his moral rectitude, his unswerving integrity. His religious fervor, too, which is a real source of his strength.[13]

Even though Colonel Qadhdhafi has become a public figure, exposed to all sorts of systems of government and ideologies, he remains constant in his religious devotion and strict observance. His early Qur'anic education has remained the main framework of his thought and actions throughout the stages of his ideological and political career. The discipline which he imposed on the Central Committee of the Unionist Free Officers is indicative of his religious and moral orientation. They were to observe prayers, in congregation whenever possible, under all circumstances. They were to abstain strictly from drinking, gambling and all other frivolous activities. He especially singled out card-playing because it could lead to actual gambling, and because it is an addictive activity. In short, strict adherence to Islam with all its moral demands constituted his code.

The group had to maintain a high degree of *esprit de corps* socially, politically and financially. There were no membership dues; rather, the pay of each member, as well as his car if he had one, were at the disposal of the group. Matters had always to be decided only when complete consensus could be achieved. Thus the absence of any member of the group invalidated the meeting. This naturally created many hardships, as the meetings of the group were held in strict secrecy. For this reason the absence of any member without a legitimate cause was severely reprimanded.

In the eyes of his colleagues, and, indeed, of the young men and women of his people, Mu'ammar embodies the spirit of their revolution, their dreams and vitality; but above all, he is 'the trustee of their liberty'.[14] The example on which Qadhdhafi modelled his political thinking, and which he instilled into the group of young officers, was that of Gamel Abdul Nasser. Nasser embodied the aspirations of all Arabs, whom he fired with his call to unity and national dignity. At first Captain Sulayman Mahmud, one of Qadhdhafi's colleagues, observed that the Unionist Free Officers thought themselves and their country, with its small and largely illiterate population, incapable of a revolution like that of Egypt. 'In fact', Sulayman reflected 'Qadhdhafi at that time tried to do no more than make us think about current affairs in the Arab World, to make us remember our origin and descent, and our subsequent history.' At that initial stage, Qadhdhafi did not speak of any direct action. It was, rather, a necessary stage of preparation, of creating in his colleagues the political awareness, discipline and dedication requisite for the success of any revolutionary movement. Sulayman continued: 'He guided our minds and led us quite naturally to the next phase, when he would enlist our services for the revolution itself.'[15]

Colonel Qadhdhafi regards Islam as a complete civilization the soul of which is its faith in the One God. If Nasser, therefore, served as an immediate model for his revolutionary dreams, he considered the glorious past of Muslim history his goal and trust. He would say, Sulayman recalled, 'Remember the greatness of our past, the grandeur of our Islamic civilization, which once extended from China to France, with, as its single impetus, our faith in God, our faith in justice, in equality and the brotherhood of mankind. If we have lost all this, it is simply because our leaders deserted the true path, because they became divided: here is the true cause of our mortification and of our humiliation. Instead of looking upon Islam as the leaven of our minds and souls we have, in our contacts with other countries, allowed it to become the means of our submission, the cause of our backwardness.' Sulayman concluded, 'Well then, imagine a caravan lost in the desert. Qadhdhafi is just the sort of man who could bring it safely to its destination.'[16]

It is, in our view, necessary to have dwelt at such length on Qadhdhafi's character, his ideals, dreams and aspirations. This is because the purpose of this work is not only to present Qadhdhafi in the light of his faith, but also to study his ideas, ideals and social vision in the light of this faith. Having thus achieved the first objective of our study, we shall now discuss the revolution of 1 September, not as a historical event but rather as the fulfilment of a dream, the fruit of a long and arduous struggle, and a concrete statement of Colonel Qadhdhafi's faith.

The 'al-Fatih' Revolution

Colonel Qadhdhafi distinguishes sharply between a revolution and a *coup d'état*.[17] A *coup d'état* is at best a change of regime, although more often than not it is simply a transfer of power from one dictatorial group to another. A revolution is, in contrast, a total reorganization of society according to new plans and ideals. In other words, a true revolution is, as the term implies, the return to a new beginning in the history of a nation.

The Libyan revolution of 1 September 1969 has been one of the most unusual of our time. It is at once internal and international, traditional and novel in its demands for reform. Its title itself expresses the symbol, meaning and goal of the revolution. '*Al-fatih*' literally means the 'opener' or 'conqueror'. It is the opening, or ushering in, of a new era. It is, in the view of the Colonel and his fellow officers, the conquering of backwardness, ignorance, national impotence and poverty. '*Al-fatih*' is one of those Qur'anic terms which are fraught with meaning, signifying military, social, pedagogical and spiritual conquest or achievement. The first, or opening day (*fatih*) of September, from which the revolution takes its name, is not simply a special national day for the Libyan people. It is the day of a new dawn of their history, a day that will never end. This notion is dramatically expressed in the slogan '*al-fatih abadan*' (al-fatih for ever).

The day of a revolution is a moment of profound and far-reaching consequences in the life of a people. It is lived with great intensity both before and after its appearance on the horizons of a nation's history. Before its appearance, the great day of a revolution is lived with anticipation, fear and hope. It brings with it promises, objectives and new national and international challenges which continue so long as the revolution itself continues to unfold. It is these three aspects of *al-fatih* revolution – namely, anticipation, promises and objectives – which will occupy us in the rest of this chapter. This is because our concern in this volume is with ideas and ideals, with concepts and attitudes rather than with economic and social issues and achievements. We shall, moreover, let Colonel Qadhdhafi tell his own story of the revolution and announce himself the objectives and promises which the revolution made to the people.

Before the revolution, Libya was ruled by King Idris, a member of the illustrious Sanusi family which founded the Sanusiyah Sufi order, and which in turn played a very important role in the history of Libya, especially during its struggle for independence. Before the discovery of oil in 1959, Libya was one of the poorest countries in the world. Yet the new oil wealth did not markedly improve the living standards of the people. It only created a small and privileged class of members of the royal family and a few of the King's most trusted friends. The King himself was a malleable instrument in the hands of Britain and the United States, and corruption was rife at all levels of government.

Like corrupt rulers everywhere, King Idris was most afraid of his own people. Thus he relied for the protection of his life and throne not on his country's armed forces, but on British and American troops. America had on the outskirts of Tripoli its largest military establishment outside the United States, Wheelus Air Base. The British likewise had a large naval base in Tubruq. For Mu'ammar al-Qadhdhafi the presence of foreigners on Libyan soil was the cause of all the ills of Libya, as has already been observed. One of the main aims of the revolution was, therefore, the liberation of the country from foreign domination.

'One day in 1963', a colleague of Qadhdhafi related, 'we were both of us at Khums, near the sea, watching the British ships anchor out there, and Qadhdhafi said to me, "That sea was once an Arab sea; and it will become Arab again one day, believe me"!'[18]

One of the first achievements of the revolution was to liberate the two bases. The American Wheelus Air Base, and the British base at Tubruq were appropriately renamed after the great warrior of early Islam, Uqbah bin Nafi, and Gamel Abdul Nasser respectively. The former was later renamed Mu'aytiqah, after a woman who fell in the struggle to liberate the base.

The years preceding the revolution were filled with activity, with fear and hope, with doubt and certainty, with trust and mistrust. The vast economic interests of Britain and the United States made it necessary for these two powers to have a large network of spies, both of their own personnel and of Libyan informers. Although the Unionist Free Officers were able to recruit large numbers of young men in the army and security police for the cause, there was always the fear that some might be informers, or others too weak and indecisive or ideologically not yet ready for the struggle. It was therefore felt that the period of preparation and waiting could not be prolonged indefinitely. Already some people were becoming too exhausted by the pressures of the secrecy and fear accompanying any underground movement.

It was therefore decided that 12 March 1969 would be the date for the final takeover of power. That night, however, the famous Egyptian singer Umm Kulthum was to give one of her all-night recitals in Benghazi. Many of the officers and other important persons who would be arrested were sure to be in the audience, and this would have led to unnecessary bloodshed. It was thus decided to postpone the date to 24 March, twelve days later. Just before that date, however, King Idris decided to go to his fortress palace at Tubruq, and army officers feared that the group had been found out and the revolution thwarted. Qadhdhafi admitted later that, 'for a moment we even thought of going to attack the King's refuge. However, we finally abandoned this idea for fear of claiming too many victims among the Tripoli police.'[19] Other dates were fixed and abandoned, just days before the actual revolution of 1 September took place.

Colonel Qadhdhafi reflects in his memoirs, written after the revolution, on the mood of the group on 31 August, the last day before the 1 September revolution. It was a long day, filled with doubts and expectations, and trust and mistrust of army personnel, soldiers as well as officers. 'A long day it was, with fears of failure, of execution, of information having reached both the government authorities and foreign powers, and of British troops having landed in large numbers in Tubruq to protect the King. The worries of the last ten years were concentrated in this one day. Yet there was no time to wait. Secrecy and underground work had exhausted the determination of many hearts.'[20] In their excitement, the officers forgot to eat, only noticing the time for the sunset prayers, which they offered in congregation.

Until the last moments before 2.30 a.m., which was the time fixed for the start of the revolution, there were many doubts. One of the group warned Qadhdhafi against starting anything, claiming that their plan had already been discovered. Yet the moment had come, and there was no turning back. It was only after the sunset prayers, however, that Colonel Qadhdhafi sat down to write the final communiqués which were to assign duties for the seizure of army barracks and official government buildings.

As Mu'ammar al-Qadhdhafi and a close colleague, Mustafa al-Kharrubi, were anxiously waiting for the decisive moment, they were listening to Radio Cairo concluding its programmes. Mustafa suggested, 'Let us seek a good omen in the verses from the Qur'an with which this station ends its broadcast.' The verses recited were:

They receive glad tidings in God's favor and bounty, for
God shall not cause the reward of the people of faith to be
lost – those who have answered the call of God and the
Apostle after they had suffered injury. For those among
them who have performed good deeds and fear God shall be
a great reward. These are they to whom people said, 'Men
have gathered against you, fear them, therefore'! Yet this
only increased them in faith, and they said, 'God is
sufficient for us, and the best of guardians is He'! Thus they
returned with grace from God and with bounty, and no evil
touched them. They sought the pleasure of God, for surely
God is the dispenser of great bounty. (Qur'an 3: 171–174)

Thus reassured, Qadhdhafi observed: 'These verses established peace and tranquility in our hearts, and we began to repeat, "God is sufficient for us, and the best of guardians is He"! We were as certain of success as though someone had come from the unknown to assure us of it.'[21]

As the zero hour drew near, Mustafa al-Kharrubi again suggested that they both perform their ablutions and offer two units (*rak'ahs*) of prayers before beginning their task. The hour did come, and success was achieved! Qadhdhafi comments on this great moment in his career and his country's history thus: 'The clock struck 2.30 and with its last moments a corrupt and backward era came to an end, and a new era began.'[22]

A revolution is a long dream until it actually happens; then it becomes a great awakening. The dream is of a brighter future, of justice and equality, but above all, it is of the security of a roof, of bread, health care and universal education for the people and their children. I once asked a simple driver in Tripoli what he thought of the revolution. His answer was direct, real and instructive. 'Why should I not support the revolution', he said, 'when before I lived in a tin shack which was like an oven in summer and an ice box in winter? Before we had hardly enough to eat. But now if my salary is not enough to take care of my family, the government gives me more. Now I live in my own house.'

The ideals and objectives of the revolution, which are our main concern in this study, were announced by Qadhdhafi himself on Libyan radio, which was taken two hours after the start of the revolution. With a firm and confident voice Colonel Mu'ammar al-Qadhdhafi delivered the first proclamation to the people on behalf of the Revolutionary Command Council. He said:

> Great people of Libya! In response to your iron will for self
> determination; in fulfillment of your precious aspirations;
> in answer to your incessant call for change and purification;
> heeding your urging to action and to initiative, to revolution
> and decisive action, your armed forces have accomplished
> the overthrow of a reactionary, backward and rotten regime
> – whose stench once disgusted us, and the sight of whose
> corrupt machinations caused our hair to stand on end.
> Thus, with one stroke from your heroic army, idols fell and
> were destroyed. In one fatal and awesome moment, the
> darkness of the ages was dispelled – first Turkish
> domination, then Italian oppression, and finally the era of
> reactionary reign, the reign of bribery and personal favors,
> the reign of treachery and transgression. From this moment
> onward, Libya shall be a free and self-governing republic.
> She shall be known as 'The Arab Libyan Republic'. She
> shall, with God's help, rise to new heights and confidently
> advance along the road of liberty, unity and social justice.
> She shall guarantee the right of all her citizens to equality,
> throwing wide open before them the doors of honest
> employment. There shall be no more people suffering
> exploitation, injustice, or oppression. Nor will there be any
> longer masters and servants. Rather, all shall be free,

21

brothers in a society over which, with God's help, the
banner of prosperity and equality shall proudly fly.[23]

The Colonel then reminded the people of the 'holy struggle' of
'Umar al-Mukhtar against Italian colonialism, as well as the struggle
of other national heroes who led the battle against other oppressive
foreign powers. He called on the people of the desert, the countryside and the cities to forget their hostilities and unite in restoring
their dignity. Qadhdhafi also reassured foreign residents, promising
that their lives and properties would be under the protection of the
armed forces. He also declared that the revolution was solely a
Libyan affair, and was not directed against any country or any
international law or treaty.

It was observed earlier in this discussion that the revolution of
1 September has been a unique phenomenon in our time. The
uniqueness of the Libyan revolution lies not so much in its short-
term promises, but rather in its overall long-term objectives. These
were proclaimed in the first communiqué issued by the Revolutionary Command Council. They fall into two categories, those dealing
with the country, its ills and its future, and others aimed at the
countries of the Third World. They were as follows:

(1) All legislative councils of the old regime are
abolished. . . .

(2) The Council of the Revolution is the only body
entitled to administer the affairs of the Libyan Arab
Republic. . . .

(3) The Council of the Revolution wishes to express to
the people its will and its determination to build a
revolutionary Libya, a socialist Libya, rooted in its own
characteristics and rejecting all doctrine, confident in the
reality of historical progress which will turn Libya, now
underdeveloped and badly governed, into a progressive
country which will fight against colonialism and racism and
will help colonized countries.

(4) The Council of the Revolution attaches great
importance to the unity of the countries of the Third World
and to all efforts directed towards the overcoming of social
and economic underdevelopment.

(5) It believes profoundly in the freedom of religion and

in the moral values contained in the Qur'an, and it promises
to defend these and to uphold them.

Qadhdhafi, as has already been observed, distinguishes
revolution from military *coup d'état*. A revolution is a commitment
to a system of ideas and ideals, and to the process of implementing
them. The three fundamental ideals of the revolution were likewise
announced by the Revolutionary Command Council on the first day
of the revolution. They were liberty, unity and socialism. These
ideals were defined as follows. 'By liberty, we mean that individual
and national liberty which will eliminate poverty, colonialism and
the presence on our soil of foreign troops and foreign bases. By
unity, we mean the unity of all the Arab people, be this in the form
of a single great Arab government or of a federation of small
governments. All will depend on circumstance. By socialism, we
mean above all an Islamic socialism. We are a Muslim nation. We
shall therefore respect, as commanded in the Qur'an, the principle
of private property, even of hereditary property.'[24]

The first principle of liberty – namely, liberty from foreign
occupation and influence – was the first task which Colonel
Qadhdhafi, as the leader of the revolution, was to undertake. After
long and arduous negotiations with the British, their base was
transferred to the Libyan armed forces on 31 March 1970. Similar
negotiations with the American government resulted in the withdrawal of all American troops from the Wheelus Air Base on 11
June of the same year.

Long after the end of the Italian colonization of Libya, all important economic affairs remained in the hands of Italian nationals
living in the country. Thus in October 1970 the state confiscated all
Italian properties, and ordered the repatriation of all Italian
nationals. Henceforth, Italians rendering any services to Libya had
to work under limited contracts with the state. Subsequently the
state took over all oil companies, except British Petroleum, which
was nationalized outright. Thus at last Libya became totally independent: militarily, economically, intellectually and socially.
Soon after the revolution, the Arabic language became the sole
medium of education and communication at all levels of Libyan
society. Tripoli after the revolution became a Muslim city, with
night-clubs closed, the drinking of alcohol banned and prostitution
eliminated.

The ideal of Arab unity remains to this day the dream and

challenge of Mu'ammar al-Qadhdhafi. Within months of the start of the revolution, he launched a determined, but so far fruitless, effort to lay the foundations of Arab unity. First, it was the Tripoli Pact, concluded between Qadhdhafi, Nasser and Numeiri, and aimed at a complete merger of the three countries, Libya, Egypt and Sudan. Nasser died in September 1970. In November of the same year, the Syrian president Hafiz al-Asad asked to be included in the Tripoli Pact. Qadhdhafi met in Cairo with Sadat and Numeiri to revive the agreement. Without Nasser, however, the plan could not be brought to fruition, in spite of subsequent meetings between the three leaders. A union of only Libya, Egypt and Syria was then formed in September 1971, after a general plebiscite in which the people of all three countries participated, but this union also was not implemented. On 18 July 1972, and after many inconclusive negotiations for an Egyptian, Libyan and Syrian union, a large demonstration demanding Arab unity set out across Libya to the Egyptian border. This effort was, however, no more than a popular expression of hope. Still another abortive attempt was made in 1974 to achieve a North African union between Libya and Tunisia in what was to be an 'Arab Islamic Republic' as a prelude to total Arab unity. Qadhdhafi's dream of Arab unity is a hope shared by all Arab people. Even Arab rulers, although in principle opposed to it because it threatens their personal power, still pay lip-service to these popular aspirations.

Against all odds both at home and abroad, Qadhdhafi has begun to reap the fruits of his ideals in his own country. Libyan society today is far more secure and affluent than at any time in recent history. It is a self-governing society, exercising control over political authority, national wealth and armaments. Popular control over political authority, national wealth and armaments are, in Qadhdhafi's view, the three most important components of freedom. We shall therefore discuss them at some length in the next chapter.

As leader of the revolution, Qadhdhafi's personality has become an integral part of the revolution in all its aspects. Yet in the end, it is the revolution, its achievements, hopes and failures, which matter. Whether the promise of the revolution is capable of realization in full or in part cannot now be judged; it is for history to record. The task of this study is to follow the progress of Mu'ammar al-Qadhdhafi's thought, and particularly its religious dimensions. It is his religious ideas and convictions, and their interpretations and implementations which stand behind all his other thoughts and actions. Yet because Qadhdhafi's political ideology is in large measure a concrete reflection of his religious temperament and convictions, some attention must be given to his political, social and economic theory as contained in *The Green Book*, to which we shall now turn.

Notes

1 Ibn Khaldun, *The Muqaddimah*, trans. Franz Rosenthal, 2nd edn., 3 vols. (Princeton, N.J., Princeton University Press, 1967), vol. 1, pp. 259–60.
2 1 Kings 19:12.
3 Qur'an 2:25.
4 Qur'an 30:24.
5 Mirella Bianco, *Gadafi, Voice from the Desert*, trans. Margaret Lyle (Paris, Editions Stock, 1975), p. 4.
6 *Ibid.*, p. 7.
7 *Ibid.*, pp. 4–5.
8 *al-Sijill al-Qawmi* (writings, speeches, and pronouncements of Mu'ammar al-Qadhdhafi, appearing in yearly volumes under various auspices), vol. 8 (1976–77), p. 90.
9 *Ibid.*, p. 91.
10 Bianco, *Gadafi*, p. 4.
11 *Ibid.*, p. 7.
12 *Ibid.*, p. 15.
13 *Ibid.*, p. 30.
14 These words are often chanted by young Libyans in the popular song '*Jamahiriyah Sultah Sha'biyah*' (Government of the Masses – Popular Power).
15 Bianco, *Gadafi*, p. 35.
16 *Ibid.*, p. 37.
17 *al-Sijill al-Qawmi*, vol. 8 (1976–77), p. 89.
18 Bianco, *Gadafi*, p. 9.
19 *al-Sijill al-Qawmi*, vol. 8, p. 101.
20 *Ibid.*, pp. 159–60.
21 *Ibid.*, p. 168.
22 *Ibid.*, p. 169.
23 *Ibid.*, vol. 1 (1969–70), pp. 9–10.
24 Bianco, *Gadafi*, p. 67.

2
Qadhdhafi's Vision: *The Green Book*

Few philosophers, social theorists or religious thinkers have had the good fortune to experiment with their ideas and ideals in real life. It should be recalled that when Plato attempted to realize his vision of the perfect republic he was sold into slavery by those who invited him to make of their state a model society, just and virtuous. Yet the Greek ideal of virtue, humanism and democracy lives on and has helped shape both Western Christian and Islamic civilizations. Qadhdhafi's *Green Book* harkens again and again to the model of popular democracy of the early Greek city-state.

Qadhdhafi's *Green Book*, unlike *The Republic*, is not the blueprint of a Utopian society waiting to be put into effect, but rather is itself the product of a revolution which has radically transformed Libyan society. Therefore, in order to understand the vision of the new society which *The Green Book* advocates, it is necessary to look at Libya before and after the revolution. Thus as background to our discussion of *The Green Book*, we shall take a cursory look at the social and economic life in Libya from 1951, when the country gained its independence, to the appearance of the first volume of *The Green Book* in 1976.

Libya before The Green Book

Among the countries of North Africa, Libya especially endured long and brutal periods of foreign domination. By the time it attained its independence on 24 December 1951, Libya had lived through three decades of Italian occupation and almost a decade of

French and British administrative rule. The kingdom of Libya then consisted of three federated provinces, covering 1,768,000 square kilometres, but with a population of only 2.5 million people. The three provinces were Cyrenaica in the east with its capital Benghazi, Tripoli in the west with Tripoli as its capital, and Fezzan in the south. These were important self-contained tribal and demographic regions.

Libya in 1951 was so poor and underdeveloped that it barely subsisted on Western aid in return for its unrestricted use by the United States and Britain as a strategic military base. King Muhammad Idris, the grandson of the founder of the Sanusiyah Sufi order, was an inept and ineffectual ruler. His seventeen-year-long reign was plagued with social instability, tribal conflict and political rivalry. In seventeen years eleven cabinets were appointed and dismissed by the King. The reason for this political instability was the rivalry between the cabinet and the powerful royal *diwan*. The King was himself more committed to the interests of his family, on whose religious prestige his own power rested, and those of Cyrenaica, which was his power base, than to general state affairs. Nevertheless, in 1963, the federation was dissolved in favour of a united country.

In foreign policy, the King was reluctant to support Arab causes directly, but allied himself closely to the West, especially Britain and the United States. He did so because he was afraid of revolutionary or radical ideas which had led to the Egyptian revolution of 1952 and which, he feared, might lead to his own downfall.

Libyan society before the revolution was largely tribal and parochial in nature. Thus any form of participation in public life was based not on the interest of the society at large, but on personal, family clan or tribal interests. The last stages of monarchical rule were, therefore, marked by unchecked corruption, nepotism, mal-administration and fiscal dishonesty.[1]

Libya is 90 per cent desert. This fact, coupled with scarce underground water resources, uncertain rainfall and inadequate methods of irrigation, mean that only 1 per cent of its vast territory was deemed economically cultivable. Yet the mainstay of Libya's economy before the flow of oil revenues in 1960 was agriculture and animal husbandry. The rate of per capita income was then $30 per annum. This picture, however, changed dramatically after the discovery of oil, when Libya became the world's fourth largest exporter of crude oil. But with oil wealth, agriculture was left to stagnate, and Libya remained a rich but economically under-developed country.[2]

Libyan society, as has already been observed, is structured around the family, clan and tribe. Such a closely knit social structure, buttressed by time honoured religious traditions and values, fosters conservative and parochial attitudes in society which impede change of any kind. These religious and social values are in themselves positive, and make for social cohesion, social morality, concern and cooperation. But they could also be used by un-scrupulous religious and tribal leaders as powerful means of con-trolling society, and thus serve their own narrow and personal interests. In fact, religious leaders before the revolution played a crucial role in the political, social and educational life of society. They headed many advisory councils, and were generally looked up to for spiritual guidance and worldly wisdom. It has been noted that religion has served as a political symbol of crucial importance in controlling and mobilizing the masses throughout Libyan history, and particularly under the monarchy.[3]

Education in Libya before the revolution was traditional. It was, moreover, limited mainly to the religious sciences. In Libya, as in many other countries of the Muslim world, this narrow approach to education has been an obstacle to modernization and progress. It has tended to professionalize Islam and to deprive it of its true character as a universal faith and social order.

During the Italian occupation, secular education was restricted to the primary grades for Libyans, where Italian was the sole medium of instruction. There were few secondary schools, even after in-dependence, and these were for boys only. University education had to be acquired abroad, in Europe or in Egypt. Before 1959, there were in Libya only twenty-five secondary school teachers and fourteen university graduates. In that year, however, the first graduating class of thirty-one students received their degrees from Qar Yunus, the only Libyan university at the time.[4] After 1959, although there remained no material obstacle in the way of pro-viding universal education for all Libyan citizens, the situation remained virtually the same until the revolution. This was to a large extent due to the fact that King Idris, who owed his power to his religious background, showed little interest in the secular demands of today's world.

Until the revolution, Libyan traditional society was 90 per-cent illiterate. The sudden oil wealth, which was largely concentrated in the two cities of Tripoli and Benghazi, attracted a huge influx from the countryside, thus further aggravating an already critical social and educational situation. The sharp decline of agriculture resulting from such mass movements from the countryside to the cities as well as the urban problem they created, prepared the ground for radical change. Thus the social transformation which *al-fatih* revolution brought about was achieved without any bloodshed or appreciable opposition.

In their first manifesto of the revolution, Mu'ammar al-Qadhdhafi and his fellow officers called the regime of King Idris a 'reactionary, backward and rotten regime'.[5] Thus from the start, the revolution aimed at completely eradicating the old order and setting up instead a new order governed by the ideals of liberty, unity and socialism. Qadhdhafi later outlined the social aims of *al-fatih* revolution in these words: 'We do not envisage a revolution which would bring to power military men, rulers, sultans, or kings. Nor will any group of people organized in any political form – be it party, class, tribe, or family – be allowed to rule over the people. On the contrary, all these symbols [of authority] have been in our view, hindrances to the realization of complete democracy for the masses.'[6]

The material achievements of the revolution in agriculture, industry, education and social welfare are beyond the scope of this study. Our concern is with the ideas and principles on which the revolution was based, and which finally crystallized in *The Green Book*. It may be asked, was *The Green Book* the expression of a Utopian ideal which Qadhdhafi dreamed up independently from *al-fatih* revolution, or was it born out of the experience of the revolution? It will be seen from the following analysis that the revolution itself was an experiment with ideas and ideals represented in many modern revolutionary movements, notably the socialist and nationalist ideals and aspirations of the Egyptian revolution. Yet while Nasser considered Islam a useful 'circle' of millions of people which cannot be ignored,[7] for Qadhdhafi religion in general, and Islam in particular, is an essential component of human natural law, and hence freedom.[8]

The young officers who planned and executed the revolution, including Mu'ammar al-Qadhdhafi himself, did not at first adopt any coherent and unified theory. Rather, their aim was primarily to establish true democracy where the people, all the people, were masters of their own destiny. Their guiding principles were those of socialist democracies as found in Marxist ideologies. During this first and formative stage of the revolution, 1969 to 1975, the goal was to achieve a good alliance or cooperation among the active elements of the people. The goal was not to establish the rule of absolute authority of the people, as embodied in *The Green Book*. Thus *The Green Book* belongs to the second stage of the revolution – that is, after 1975 – although in 1973 the basic idea of *The Green Book*, namely, the establishment of the authority of the people, had already been declared.[9]

The Libya of *al-fatih* revolution was declared, in a constitutional communiqué given shortly after the revolution, as a modern socialist state whose primary aims were to achieve social justice, and to abolish all forms of exploitation. It was further stressed that the country's constitution, as well as all other laws, should be based on the humanistic values of the Islamic Arab heritage. The special circumstances and character of the Libyan people would also be taken into consideration.[10] These two frames of reference – the Islamic Arab heritage and the peculiar character and circumstances of the Libyan people – provide the actual framework for *The Green Book*, even though it purports to be universal in its scope and purpose.

It may be further argued that all the major ideas of *The Green Book* were anticipated in the new laws governing Libyan society after the revolution. One such law, promulgated on 26 September 1969, prohibits using labourers as though they were commodities for trade. *The Green Book*, as we shall see, carried this further by insisting that workers must be partners and not wage earners. On 8 November of the same year, strict laws were put into effect regulating the rent of business establishments. *The Green Book* went so far in safeguarding the rights of the workers as to insist that the basic needs of the people could not be controlled by individuals.

The Green Book insisted that the wealth of society must be controlled by all the people. Thus any personal wealth which cannot be proven to be the legitimate surplus of lawfully earned wealth must be returned to the people. This principle was anticipated in the decision of the government in July 1970 to investigate and confiscate, when necessary, all properties which were found to be illegally acquired. In June of the following year the properties of certain suspected individuals were placed under direct government supervision.[11] It must, however, be observed that the conservative and traditional nature of Libyan society, especially its wealthy

segments, impeded progress in implementing these and other programmes such as land reforms and the redistribution of ill-gotten
wealth.[12]

It may be seen from our brief examination of pre-revolutionary
Libya in this and the previous chapter that under the monarchy it
was a completely *laissez-faire* country economically and politically.
Thus one of the first tasks of the revolution was to promote social
cohesion and cooperation. In its first constitutional manifesto,
therefore, the Revolutionary Command Council declared: 'Social
cohesion is the foundation of national unity.' Yet true social
cohesion meant that 'All citizens are equal before the law'. The
state undertook to guarantee the social rights of its citizens.[13]

After the revolution Libya was a one-party state. It was not the
people in general who exercised political authority, but only the
Arab Socialist Union. Yet even then it was felt that political parties
had no place in Libya. In 1972, a law (number 71) concerning
political parties was implemented. This law regarded the organization of, and affiliation with, any political party to be a crime and
betrayal of the authority of the people, who are represented in the
Arab Socialist Union.[14] In a famous address which Colonel
Qadhdhafi delivered in the traditional city of al-Bayd' in the
celebrations of the withdrawal of British forces from Libya, on 8
April 1970, he decisively declared: 'There shall be no parties,
affiliations or schisms. Partisan affiliation shall be regarded as high
treason because it leads to the disintegration of national unity.' He
further argued, 'It is imperative that we safeguard the national unity
which is natural for the homogenous Libyan people. We must be
"one rank like a well compacted edifice".'[15]

We have so far spoken of Libya from independence to revolution.
For the sake of closer analysis, the history of the revolution may
itself be divided into three phases. The first and formative phase,
with which we have been thus far concerned, extends from 1
September 1969 to the 15 April 1973. The second, which coincides
with the appearance of *The Green Book*, extends from 15 April
1973 to 2 March 1977. The third phase is what may be termed as the
post-*Green Book* phase, which is still unfolding, and which will be
for later history to record.

During the second phase Mu'ammar al-Qadhdhafi's ideas began
to take final shape and also to be implemented. This period saw the
rise of the *jamahiriyah* (populist) society of the masses. It witnessed
the organization of the people's congresses, committees, unions

and syndicates.

At Zwarah on 15 April 1973, the Prophet's birthday, Qadhdhafi announced his 'historic' five points. They were:

(1) The abolition of all laws which were in force, and substitution for them of laws made by the people and based on Islamic precepts;

(2) the purge from the country of all 'sick people', the deviationists who did not fully participate in the revolution, but instead sought to subvert it by the importation of foreign and alien ideas;

(3) the declaration that to the people, all the people, belonged absolute freedom, and no freedom for the enemies of the people;

(4) the carrying of the revolution into the administrative sector, or the cumbersome government bureaucracy; and

(5) the declaration of a cultural revolution against all foreign books and ideas which mislead the people and make them doubt their own Islamic and Arab heritage.[16]

It is this 'cultural revolution', the relentless effort to remodel the thinking of the people along revolutionary lines, which is the most prominently visible aspect of the revolution to the outside world. The speech at Zwarah, is crucial for the understanding of the revolution – not only its ideas but also its tone, impact and character. We shall, therefore, quote at some length excerpts from this important address:

O you people, tear to shreds all imported books which do not set forth [the values of] the Arab heritage [*al-'urubah*] and of Islam, of socialism and of progress.

By socialism Qadhdhafi means a system based on the Qur'an, and not on a Marxist or any imported socialist ideology. This is an important point to which we shall return. He continues:

O you people, destroy all libraries and other bookhouses out of which the true light does not shine forth, the light which guides the people and leads them 'out of the darkness and into the light' [Qur'an 2:257]. But support those other things, that which is authentic, that which the people want and which pleases God, and thus must remain. O you people, burn and destroy all the curricula which do not express the truth, curricula which stuff our brains with shallow subjects. Destroy the curricula which were designed during the reactionary regime, curricula which colonialism intruded with hidden hands into our country. The masses are, after this day, no longer in need of any deceiving hypocritical intermediaries, whether they carry the Gospel, the Qur'an, communism, capitalism, or any other theory. The masses have no need for the deception of the right or of the left! The masses today are in need of destroying their fetters, of governing themselves, and of building their own future according to their own will. Down with any branch of knowledge which cannot be placed in the service of the people! For it is not true knowledge.[17]

It was such calls upon the people to exercise their authority over their own lives and destiny which, in our view, led to the concept of 'direct democracy'. This concept is basic to Qadhdhafi's Third Universal Theory. It is embodied in the popular congresses, committees and other such power organs of the people.

On 4 June 1973, less than two months after the Zwarah address, Colonel Qadhdhafi called on the people to take over the radio and television stations of the country. These are, in the Colonel's view, important means of communication which must, therefore, be placed in the service of the revolution. The next day he went himself to supervise the takeover, and to ensure a smooth transition from commercial to revolutionary administration.[18]

If public rallies and other means of showing popular commitment to the revolution, and the will to defend it, are indicative of success, then the revolution has indeed been successful. In Libya today there are no strikes, riots or demonstrations. The economy has been totally socialized. The tribal structure of society has been completely transformed. Even the practice of Islam, focusing on the personality of the Prophet Muhammad has been challenged and largely redirected so as to centre on the Qur'an as the 'sacred law' (*shari'ah*) of society.[19]

It was noted earlier that the main aim of the revolution has been the establishment of the people's authority on all levels of society. By 'the people' is here meant every individual, whatever his or her social, economic or intellectual status in society may be. Thus the second phase of the revolution culminated in an important public gathering of popular congresses and popular committees in Sabha held from 28 February to 2 March 1977, to coincide with the Prophet's birthday. In that historic public gathering an important document affirming the absolute authority of the people was adopted. It was in that meeting as well that Libya was declared 'The Socialist People's Libyan Arab Jamahiriya'.[20]

Let it be recalled that this historic gathering was held in Sabha, in the heart of the desert, where the idea of the revolution was born.[21] In fact the philosophy of *The Green Book*, the 'Third Universal Theory', was itself worked out in the desert. Three years earlier, in April 1974, Mu'ammar al-Qadhdhafi relinquished his job as the leader of the country and became instead *Qa'id al-Thawrah* (Leader of the Revolution). This decision was not only proper, but it was also necessary given the logic of the Third Universal Theory, which calls for a society without leaders and followers. It was for this reason that with the establishment of the *jamahiriyah*, or populist society of the masses, the Revolutionary Command Council was dissolved by a resolution of the Third Popular Congress.

Qadhdhafi's role is now bound with that of *The Green Book*. However, neither he nor *The Green Book* have any binding authority on the people, at least officially, but both are accepted as guides to a new and controversial if not unique experiment in social living. Having surveyed briefly the history of the Revolution until the appearance of *The Green Book*, we shall now examine *The Green Book* itself.

The Green Book 1: Solving the Problem of Democracy

Mu'ammar al-Qadhdhafi is a simple son of the desert, a man of deep religious faith and a humanist. That there is a real tension between Qadhdhafi's faith and ideology or humanism is clearly manifest in all his words and actions. It is a tension among these three decisive elements in his character. All three elements, moreover, are expressed in his ideal of human freedom, which he preaches with obsessive devotion, and which forms the main subject of his only formal writing, *The Green Book*. This brief and cryptic treatise is divided into three parts. The first endeavours to offer the ultimate solution to the problem of democracy. It purports to be a guide for the political liberation of human societies from outmoded and oppressive political systems. The second part, claiming to provide the solution to the economic problem, is a guide to economic freedom through a philosophy of 'new socialism'. The third and final part of *The Green Book* professes to provide the key to the social problems of humanity by advocating liberation from all human-made laws and artificial social systems and structures.

The Green Book has been no less controversial than its author. Is it, as some have thought, Qadhdhafi's answer to Chairman Mao's *Red Book*? Or is it, as others have claimed, a new scripture which is intended to supplant and supersede the Qur'an? Before analyzing each of *The Green Book*'s three parts separately, it may be well to observe how the author himself has characterized it.

The Green Book, Qadhdhafi asserted, is like any other book which advocates a new socio-economic theory or philosophy. It does not have the authority of any resolution or decision of the Revolutionary Command Council. Nor is anyone obliged to implement it. It simply represents the author's political views.[22]

Qadhdhafi has always insisted that his Third Universal Theory is a common-sense interpretation of Islam. The first part of *The Green Book*, he has argued, is an interpretation of one single verse of the Qur'an: 'and their affairs are decided through consultation [*shura*] among themselves'.[23] The concept of *shura*, or consultation, has occupied a special place in every Islamic political system or ideology. It is put forth by every Islamic regime as the basis of its legitimacy. It is presented as the answer to Western democracy. To some Muslims, it simply means a consultative assembly advising an otherwise despotic ruler. To others, it means an assembly of jurists ruling over a traditional Islamic society strictly governed by the *shari'ah*. Only Qadhdhafi has taken this important Qur'anic precept seriously, understanding it literally, and applying it equally to every member of society.

Qadhdhafi begins the first part of *The Green Book* by defining the problem. It lies in the form of government (*adat al-hukm*). 'The form of government', he insists, 'is the most important problem which faces human societies.' It manifests itself at the lowest level of human relations, such as the family, as well as at the highest levels of modern nation-states. Human societies have not, in Qadhdhafi's view, succeeded in finding a final and democratic solution to this problem. He insists further that all modern forms of government are the result of a vicious struggle among earlier forms and ideologies for power. This struggle was at times peaceful, but more often violent, among social classes, political parties, religious sects and individuals. The result is always victory for one party over another, but this always means 'the defeat of the people, that is, defeat of true democracy'.[24]

This struggle reached an important stage with the rise of parliamentary democracy. Elsewhere Mu'ammar al-Qadhdhafi admitted that outside the system of direct democracy of the Third Universal Theory, freely elected representatives provide the best system of government. Still, he calls representative democracy 'a false democracy', and thus 'a rejected philosophy'.[25] A representative system of government is, for Qadhdhafi, a dictatorial rule either of the minority over the majority or vice versa. If, for example, 51 per cent of the population votes for someone and 49 per cent against him, then 49 per cent of the people would be denied their right to be represented by someone acceptable to them. Qadhdhafi, moreover, regards election campaigns as a form of demagoguery because only the rich can enter them.

One of the most popular slogans of *The Green Book* is, 'There ought to be no representation on behalf of the people; representation is a deception.' This is because, another slogan asserts, 'A representative assembly is popular rule *in absentia*.' This is again due to the fact that democracy is the direct authority of the people, not a representative authority.[26] A representative national assembly or parliament is established either through electoral districts, a political party or coalition of parties, or by appointment. In all cases, it is a false democracy because members of such an assembly represent only their party or coalition, and not the people.

We have already noted Qadhdhafi's aversion to political parties. In fact, he sees any party, be it political, religious or social, as a hindrance to progress in society. This is also true of tribal as well as religious groups or alliances. The only difference between a tribe and a party is, according to Qadhdhafi, 'that of blood ties'. Otherwise they are both made up of people having common interests. These could be education, faith or ideology. Thus such people join a party or action group not to serve the people but to achieve their own interests. Political parties are the latest form of dictatorial rule because they represent the rule of a part over the whole of society. Qadhdhafi, therefore, considers party politics as 'an abortion of democracy'.[27]

The problem of the minority rule of a party is made even worse by the multiplicity of parties. An increase in the number of political parties only contributes to the intensity and widening of the struggle for power. This party struggle for power often leads to the destruction of the bases of any achievements by the people, whether these be in the areas of social service or economic welfare. The only justification for the existence of any party lies in its ability to subvert the plans or achievements of its rival, and thus gain for itself political power.

A social class (*tabaqah*) is still another minority which has often usurped the authority of the people and their mastery over their own destiny. Like political parties, tribes or sectarian groups, a socio-economic class is a special group with common interests. None the less, Colonel Qadhdhafi prefers a class or tribal coalition to that of political parties. His reason is instructive, no doubt arising from his own social environment: 'This is because human societies are originally made up of different tribes, and it is rare to find people who have no tribe. All people, moreover, belong to different social classes.'[28]

Qadhdhafi's preference for social classes, tribes and religious sects is based on his notion of natural society. These social groups are natural because they are traditional. They are the first social structures observable in recorded human history. Thus Qadhdhafi argues that society began as one class: 'Any society in which various classes are engaged in the struggle for power must have been originally a single class. Out of this one class, however, others were born in accordance with an inexorable law of the evolution of all things.'[29] Class struggle often leads to an artificial return to the one-class structure. This is so because other classes were crushed by force, and did not disappear with the rise of the direct popular democracy of the masses. He states: 'Any class which inherits a society, inherits its characteristics as well.' Thus if the working class, for example, crushes all other classes in society, it becomes both its social and physical base from which other classes will eventually evolve. This process begins with the appearance of socially and economically privileged individuals, then special groups and finally classes. Then the struggle begins anew as different classes, groups and individuals attempt to seize power and thus impose a new dictatorship. Qadhdhafi concludes: 'all attempts to unify the physical base of society as a way of solving the problem of government, or decide the struggle in favor of a party, class, religious group, or tribe – and the attempt then to gain the approval of the masses through elections or plebiscites – all such attempts have failed. Repeating them has become a waste of time and a mockery of the masses.'[30]

According to *The Green Book*, a plebiscite is yet another form of deception. Those who say 'yes' or 'no' are not really allowed to express their opinion because they are not allowed to state the reason for their decision. This, Qadhdhafi insists, 'is the most cruel and most extreme form of repressive dictatorship'.[31] He then asks: 'What then is the way which human societies must follow if they are to rid themselves once and for all of forms of tyranny and dictatorship?'[32] The solution lies in discovering a new form of government, a government which is all the people, and not any particular group, party or class. *The Green Book* presents the final solution to this problem: 'It points the right way for human society to arrive at the society of direct democracy based on the authority of the people.'[33]

The form of government which *The Green Book* presents as an answer to the problem of democracy is that of the people's congresses and committees. Qadhdhafi declares with confidence: 'People's congresses are the only means of achieving popular democracy. All forms of government in force in the world today are non-democratic until and unless they are guided to this system. People's congresses are the end of a long journey of the masses towards democracy.'[34]

This new experiment in democracy rests on the 'direct popular authority', which was legislated in March 1977, as 'the sole foundation of the new political system in the Socialist People's Libyan Arab *Jamahiriyah*'. The new name of Libya was officially announced to the world in a full-page advertisement in the *Christian Science Monitor* on 7 April 1977.[35] The last word of this rather long name is left untranslated. It means roughly 'populist republic'. This designation is meant to distinguish the new Libya from the concept of a republican state headed by a president. In the state of the *jamahir* (multitudes or masses) everyone is master, and there are no slaves, servants or underdogs. The structure of this new society is broad and so far somewhat cumbersome. It is of course in its experimental stages.

Each municipality in the country has a number of people's congresses consonant with its population. In the country as a whole, there are ninety-seven local or basic congresses. In every municipality a basic committee is nominated to oversee the execution of the decisions and recommendations of the congresses under its supervision. A similar, but much enlarged, committee is nominated, one whose supervision extends over the country. This committee is further entrusted with foreign affairs. The executive powers of this committee cannot go beyond the decisions of the local congresses of the country as a whole on both domestic and foreign matters.[36]

The people's congresses are essentially legislative bodies. They promulgate laws and make recommendations which are passed on to the committee for execution. The committees, however, are themselves supervised by the local congresses which appoint them. Every committee appoints a general secretary and two assistant secretaries. All the secretaries are in turn members of a general national congress. A member of every organization – workers or professional unions, syndicates, student unions and the like – also represents his or her organization in the general national congress. Finally, people's committees are nominated to replace administrative government offices, departments and ministries. These committees, however, act on the decisions of the general national congress as well as those of the local congresses, and have no political authority of their own.[37]

This rather complex political structure is designed to give the opportunity to every member of society, male and female, to participate in this form of direct democracy. Meetings of the local congresses resemble the traditional New England town council meetings, and even more the meetings of the Society of Friends, the Quakers. Decisions are not arrived at through voting, but rather through general consensus. Thus often meetings go on for a long time before any decision is arrived at. This perhaps is one of the reasons why it has been so difficult actively to involve many Libyans in the system. Nevertheless, for Colonel Qadhdhafi and the ever-increasing number of his supporters, specially among the young, the price in inefficient bureaucracy and a long process of education of the masses will in the end be worth the reward. Qadhdhafi hopes that, with both the legislative and executive powers of all levels finally in the hands of all the people, 'the old and worn-out definition of democracy, . . . which claims that democracy is the people's supervision of the government, will give place to the right definition which is, "democracy is the supervision of the people of themselves" '.[38]

It has been observed that the main role of the people's congresses is to make the laws and decisions that will guide the new society in its exercise of direct popular democracy. This task is, however, not strictly legislative; its object is also to promote moral and social cohesion. Hence, the two primary sources of this social law, broadly understood, are social custom or tradition (*al-'urf*) and religion with all its laws and precepts. Social law, or what Qadhdhafi calls *shari'at al-Mujtama'* (the sacred law of society) is natural law, innately sensed by every human being. It is the *fitrah* or natural state 'in which God created humankind'.[39]

By social custom, Qadhdhafi means general social customs which become 'fundamentals governing human rights and duties, truth and falsehood, and good and evil'.[40] This natural law is not the possession or creation of any individual or group in society. It is rather 'an eternal heritage, which is not a possession of the living only'.[41] Unlike modern laws and constitutions, which *The Green Book* calls positive laws, natural social law is primordial and unchanging. Modern positive laws are, in contrast, created by particular forms of government designed to serve only their interests. Qadhdhafi writes: 'The custom, or trodden path [*sunnah*] of the dictatorial forms of government took the place of the law, or *sunnah*, of nature. Positive law replaced natural law, hence social criteria are lost'. Natural law is one, as humanity is one. A human being is a human being anywhere. He is one in his human characteristic and one in his feelings. Thus natural law came into being as a logical general law [*namus*] for all human beings as members of the one humanity. But then came positive laws which do not look at human beings as one in their humanity.[42]

Qadhdhafi has argued that dictatorial regimes and rulers moved the masses away from religion as a fundamental source of law in order that they might themselves promulgate new laws which agreed with their own interests and viewpoints. In reality they themselves should have lived by this natural law which is binding on the whole of human society, including its dictators. This process was enhanced, Qadhdhafi believes, by the repeated periods of dictatorial rule which most human societies experienced at different times in their history. Consequently, he rejects the notion of a secular state. He refuses to obey any man-made laws or constitutions.[43] He declares: 'The natural law of any society is social custom [*al-'urf*] or religion. Any attempt, therefore, to find a law for any society outside these two sources is a futile and illogical endeavor.'[44]

It was argued earlier that Mu'ammar al-Qadhdhafi is a humanist.

This can be seen from his insistence on human freedom, freedom unconditioned and unhampered by anything. Another argument which shows his humanistic tendency is that modern law and constitutional books are fraught with laws of material and physical punishment. Social custom, in contrast, is nearly free from such punishments. Social custom instead prescribes moral and social disciplines, which are more worthy of the dignity of man. Religion encompasses social custom and assimilates it. Thus even the material or physical punishments which religion prescribes are postponed till the next world. Qadhdhafi has in mind no doubt the notion of heaven and hell, and rewards and punishments as found in all three monotheistic religious traditions: Judaism, Christianity and Islam. Only in extreme cases of public immorality such as adultery, murder or theft does religion mete out harsh punishments.

The relationship of social custom with religion is a complementary one. Religion assimilates social custom, and social custom expresses the life situation of human societies. Hence, all non-religious and non-customary laws are invocations by some men against other men.

Qadhdhafi finally asks: But who can guard society against infringements of this natural law? His answer is that society must be its own keeper. This it would do through the right forms of government which would naturally arise out of this system. But if society deviates, he further asks, how is it to be corrected? This could be done, he argues, through a revolution. Qadhdhafi concedes that any revolutionary process would inevitably lead to violence as one group attempts to gain power over the rest of society. Qadhdhafi then offers an explanation of this phenomenon, without, however, justifying it. He says: 'Violence as means to bring about change in society is in itself a non-democratic action. It takes place, however, as a result of non-democratic conditions prior to it. Furthermore, a society which becomes subject to his situation is a backward society.'[45] In a self-governing society based on the Third Universal Theory, any deviation can be corrected through the democratic process.

The Green Book recognizes the role of the press in either promoting or subverting the democratic process. It thus regards as partisan and hence not free any medium of communication and information which is not controlled and operated by a committee representing the people. It further regards the problem of the freedom of the press, which remains a burning issue in today's world, as an integral part of the general problem of democracy. It will not be solved, therefore, until the entire problem of democracy is settled.[46]

The first part of *The Green Book* concludes on an impassioned note of anticipation of this new era of world history, an era of freedom and peace for all. It is a truly eschatological prediction.

> Finally the era of the masses is advancing hastily upon us,
> after the era of republics. It sets feelings ablaze, and dazzles
> sights! Yet at the same time that it announces the coming of
> true liberty for the masses, and the happy deliverance from
> the shackles of old forms of governments, it also warns of an
> era of social chaos and disintegration if the new democracy,
> which is the authority of the people is defeated and followed
> by the rule of any particular individual, class, tribe,
> confessional group, or political party.

Qadhdhafi finally admits that what he has so far presented is true democracy, but only from a theoretical point of view. 'In reality', he concludes, 'those who are strong always rule.'[47]

The Green Book 2: Solving the Economic Problem

Political freedom, as advocated by *The Green Book*, is impossible to attain without economic freedom. In fact the latter is more tangible, and in many ways more difficult to achieve. The world today is largely dominated by two powers, representing the capitalist and Marxist systems. For a better understanding of the third system which *The Green Book* presents, it is important to discuss briefly Mu'ammar al-Qadhdhafi's view of these two ideologies, and especially their economic dimensions.

The world, Qadhdhafi asserts, may from time to time exchange one system or ideology for another, but it does not in reality change. The best examples of this phenomenon are the capitalist and Marxist systems. They may appear to be different, but in reality they are 'the two faces of one coin'.[48] They both exploit the masses, regardless of whether there are many employers, as in the capitalist system, or only one employer, as in the Marxist system. It is always the workers who are paid specific wages for their labour, whether they work for private enterprise or for the state as the sole employer.

The Marxist state was established through the unlimited use of violence. This violence was used to separate man completely from his traditional life, and recondition him as a robot. Thus, as an anonymous commentator remarks,

> By simply pressing a particular button, human robots move like ants to gather the fruits of their labor into previously designated places of storage. Such human robots do not have the freedom to choose when to eat and drink, love and dream, desire and rest; to rise to a higher station in life or achieve fame.

The system subsists on violence,

> and requires that an iron fist be always placed over the head of the people. Were it possible for this iron fist to be lifted, people would revert back to their old ways and only serve their own private interests. The tendency in Marxist society is, therefore, to establish a strong state which controls the wealth, authority and arms in order for it to coerce all people to relinquish their personal interest and work only for Communism.[49]

It is inevitable that the people will, sooner or later, revolt against this system. Portents for this have already appeared in Hungary, Yugoslavia and Poland. The anonymous commentator on *The Green Book* predicts a revolution even in the Soviet Union itself in the not too distant future.

The communist and capitalist systems are similar in that both have a people, a government and a state. They both have a regular army and a police force, which are used in the capitalist system to protect the interests of rich capitalists, and in the Marxist system to protect the ruling party. Yet in both systems the people toil without being able to manage their own affairs. Rather, they are managed by public or private administrations which represent either the state, or private exploitative firms or companies. Our commentator concludes:

> Leaders of the capitalist system pride themselves on their
> system having produced some affluent workers, yet they
> ignore those who became poor because of the affluence of
> the workers who usurped their opportunities for work and
> their share of the wealth of society. Marxists, likewise, pride
> themselves on having eliminated unemployment and thus
> ensured employment opportunities for all those who are
> capable of using them, yet they too ignore their own in-
> ability to provide the comforts of life for the workers.[50]

Mu'ammar al-Qadhdhafi begins his discussion of the economic
problem with a sharp critique of all the economic systems in force in
the world today. He asserts that despite social measures such as
social security, fixing a minimum wage and regulating the number of
working hours, the right to strike, and limiting or eliminating
private ownership, a most important problem remains unsolved.
The problem is again that of true human freedom. To be sure, a
good measure of justice has been achieved through these and other
reforms. Yet the relationship of workers and technicians with pro-
ducers remains that of master and servant. All reforms and im-
provements in the relationship have been no more then half-
hearted measures, much nearer to charity than to the recognition of
the rights of the workers.

Workers are given a certain wage in return for a commodity
which they produce. They are not allowed to be the actual consumers of their products because they have sold this right for a small
wage. Whereas the right principle, Qadhdhafi argues, 'is that "he
who produces must himself be the consumer of his product".' He
thus concludes: 'However improved the lot of the workers may be,
they still remain in a way [temporary] slaves.'[51] All increases in
wages or social security are no more than charitable gifts which the
rich dole out to the workers. Only when ownership is in the hands of
all the people, managed by their congresses and committees, will
workers become 'partners and not wage earners'. The workers are
now merely servants either to the state, to rich businesses, or to the
political party which has usurped authority and wealth. 'The final
solution, therefore', Qadhdhafi argues, 'is the elimination of wage
earning, and hence the liberation of mankind from its enslavement.
It is the return to the natural principles which governed human
relations before the rise of social classes, forms of government and
[their] imposed legislation.' He further argues, 'Only natural prin-

ciples can be taken as the criteria, and the sole source and reference of human relations.'[52] These natural principles have already proved capable of creating a new socialist system which guarantees equality among all members of society. It has achieved near equality among all members of society as consumers of the products which they themselves produced. Qadhdhafi then contrasts this 'natural' approach to economics with the 'unnatural', and therefore corrupt, economies of the modern world. He writes: 'The approach which allows the exploitation by one person of another, and which allows an individual to possess more than his needs of the wealth of society, is an evident deviation from the natural principle. It is the beginning of corruption and disorientation of the life of human society.'[53]

The essential elements of production are three: raw materials, means of production and the producer. The 'natural principle' is, Qadhdhafi argues, that all those who are involved in the operation of production must have an equal share of the final product. As they are all equal in the total operation of production, so must they be also equal in their rights to the commodities produced. This natural law of production has remained unchanged from the time when men began to make simple tools, to the present, when the machine has replaced human and animal power. It remains unchanged even though a few technicians and engineers have taken the place of vast numbers of labourers. All attempts at regulating the production and distribution of industrial goods have failed because they did not recognize and follow this natural principle. The same principle also applies to agriculture, where the three elements of production are: the land, the farmer and the machine.

Qadhdhafi contends that, because of the changes brought about by the Industrial Revolution, labour unions will inevitably disappear as the need for them in large numbers continues to decline. They will be replaced by unions of technicians and engineers. 'Nevertheless', he concludes, 'man in his new form shall always remain an essential element in the task of industrial production.'[54]

This means that human beings will continue to have needs which must be fulfilled by industrial products of all kinds. Freedom, therefore, lies in freeing the essential needs of the individual from the control of others. This idea is expressed in the oft-quoted slogan: 'In need freedom resides.' *The Green Book* declares:

> The freedom of any human being is deficient to the extent that another controls his needs. Needs can lead to the

enslavement of a human being by another. Furthermore, the primary cause of exploitation is need. Thus social struggle always arises when one group in society gains control over the needs of others.[55]

Among the essential needs of the individual as well as the family is the home. A man is not free so long as he lives in the house of another, whether he pays rent or not. Hence, another popular slogan from *The Green Book* reads, 'A house belongs to its occupants.' It is not right, therefore, that a man pay rent to any agent, be it the state, a large real estate firm, or private landlord. Mu'mmar al-Qadhdhafi asserts:

No one has the right, therefore, to build any house beyond his need. This is because that house would then embody the need of another person. Building it with the intention of renting it out is the beginning of the process of controlling another person's need; yet in need freedom resides.[56]

Another essential human need is, according to *The Green Book*, 'livelihood'. Because the livelihood of any person is most essential, it must be secured. It should not be dependent on wages or charity from any other individual, group or agency. *The Green Book* states this principle with its usual terseness: 'There shall be no wage earners in a socialist society, but rather partners.' 'Brother Mu'ammar', as he is often called, then addresses each of his fellow members of the 'new society' individually, saying: 'The means of your livelihood are your own private property which you yourself must manage within the bound of satisfying your personal needs – or it must be your share of a product, in the production of which you were an essential participant – and not a wage for a labor rendered to anyone.'[57]

Another need which Qadhdhafi considers vital is *al-markub*, or means of transport. It is not allowed, therefore, in a socialist society than any individual or company controls the means of transport of others. Rather, everyone's vehicle or other means of transport must be his own property.[58]

The final example which *The Green Book* offers is the land. It belongs to no one in particular, yet every individual has the right to use it to fulfil his needs. Every individual has the right to work the land, to cultivate it or use it for pasture. This right extends to the person's heirs who inherit not the land but the right to use it.[59]

Only when the basic needs of every individual can be freed from outside control will humanity attain material, intellectual and spiritual liberty. In this new society a worker either works for himself or is an active member in a cooperative with an equal share in its yields and profits. Those who provide public services, such as physicians, nurses, teachers and the like, must have their material needs taken care of by society. In contrast with the Marxist adage, 'from each according to his ability and to each according to his need', *The Green Book* says: 'from each according to his ability and to each according to his effort'. Thus a worker has the right to set aside a portion of what he, through his own personal effort, earns to meet his material needs. But to hoard surplus wealth, even after satisfying one's material needs, is considered by Qadhdhafi as hoarding 'the need of another person of the wealth of society'.[60]

Colonel Qadhdhafi argues that workers who work for wages but have no share in what they produce have no incentive to increase their output because they are not working for themselves. Thus, he contends, production based on wage labour is 'facing continuous decline because it rests on the shoulders of wage earners'.[61]

It is an undisputed fact that not all people in society are equal in their intelligence, resourcefulness and motivation. There are those also who, because of physical or mental disabilities, are unable to provide for their needs. *The Green Book* asserts that those who are highly motivated and possessed of superior intelligence do not have the right to usurp the share of others of the wealth of society. They are, however, entitled to satisfy their needs, and to save a portion of what they have earned for this purpose. Likewise, the situation of the elderly, disabled and mentally retarded members of society does not mean that they are not entitled to the same share of the wealth of society as those who are healthy.[62]

Public wealth is compared by *The Green Book* to a storehouse. Each member of society gets what he needs in accordance with his level of excellence in the services he renders to society. This of course does not exclude the possibility of having varying levels of affluence within a society. Qadhdhafi says: 'The share of every individual in the public wealth of society varies only in accordance with the kind of public service he performs, or the excellence of the work he does.' Since needs also vary in accordance with the education and environment of each member of society, then there is in the final analysis no real standard by which wealth should be distributed. Indeed, Qadhdhafi insists the freedom can only be relevant to the extent that each individual controls and even owns the means of satisfying his needs. This personal control or ownership, Qadhdhafi calls 'a sacred right'.[63]

Qadhdhafi goes on to predict that the powers which threaten the rights of labour unions and the like will themselves contribute to the transformation of Western society of wage earners to a society of partners. The revolutionary process which will lead to this transformation begins with the ability of the workers to control their share of production. Strikes will, likewise, change from being demands for pay rises to demands for a share in production. This, he believes, will happen sooner or later as people become guided by *The Green Book*.[64]

Like most social philosophers, Qadhdhafi follows the logic of his own theory to its ideal Utopian conclusion. Since the dawn of recorded history men have used some sort of exchange of goods for portable wealth. Whether it is money, precious metals or worthless objects, buying and selling continue to be the dominant factor in the lives of human societies. Still Qadhdhafi the humanist looks forward to a time when in 'the new socialist society, profit and money shall finally disappear'. This will mean a total transformation of human society to a producing society. It will also mean that a high enough level of production will be reached to fulfil the needs of all the members of society. 'In this final stage', Qadhdhafi hopes, 'profit will spontaneously disappear, and with it will also cease the need for money.'[65]

Mu'ammar al-Qadhdhafi is more a social reformer than a philosopher. Thus he comes down from his lofty Utopian vision to a discussion of yet another class of oppressed persons: domestics and house servants. This is yet another indication of his practical concerns. To him no doubt this issue is as important as any other social or economic problem, simply because it involves people whose rights have been denied. He begins from the conviction, 'a house should be served by its inhabitants'. Starting from this conviction, he considers house servants as 'the slaves of the modern age'. They are lower in the public sector than wage labourers. Hence, he declares, 'they are in even greater need of liberation from the slavery of a society of wage earners, the society of slaves'. In situations where house servants are necessary, Qadhdhafi concedes, they must be considered as regular employees in any public company, and should like them be eligible for promotion and other social benefits and securities.[66]

As will become evident from the following discussion, and especially the next chapter, Qadhdhafi is motivated largely by Islamic principles. The Qu'ran's strict prohibition of usury, its insistence on *zakat*, or the obligatory welfare alms, and its call to the people of faith to 'spend of their wealth in the way of God', are certainly in Qadhdhafi's economic ideas. Likewise, the Qur'an and Prophetic Tradition uphold the principle of the equality of all human beings before God, and hence their humanity. This principle is the basis of Qadhdhafi's social vision. It is to this vision that we shall now turn.

The Green Book 3: Solving the Problem of Society

The third part of *The Green Book* is, in some ways, the most important and most interesting part because it is the most theoretical. It is also the most indicative exposé of Mu'ammar al-Qadhdhafi's thinking. It sets forth his basic theory in a way that illuminates the political and economic dimensions already discussed.

It has already been observed that the basic components of the structure of any society are, for Qadhdhafi, social custom (*'urf*), and religion broadly understood (*din*). *'Urf* in this discussion is translated as ethnic identity, or nationalism (*qawmiyah*). If social custom is the sum total of the customs, mores and folkways of society, then ethnic identity must be regarded as the synthesis of these elements in the history of a nation, giving it its distinct cultural and historic personality. Qadhdhafi thus begins his discussion with the declaration, 'The sole mover of human history is the social and ethnic factor. This social link forms the basic relationships among the primary units of human societies, from the family to the tribe, then the nation, which is the fundamental factor of history.'[67]

The heroes of history are its immediate movers. They are willing to sacrifice everything, even their lives, for particular causes which pertain to a people with whom they have a special relationship. This special social relationship is that between members of a nation. The causes for which these heroes struggle are thus national causes.

The primary purpose behind most of the movements of history is the independence of one society, or ethnic nation, from another. 'Thus societal movements are always independence movements,

49

movements aiming at the realization of the essential identity of a defeated or oppressed group or society by another.'[68] Modern movements are at one and the same time nationalistic as well as ethnic and societal. They are liberation movements which will persist until every ethnic group, society or nation is liberated from the control of another. 'This means,' in Qadhdhafi's view, 'that the world is now passing through a period of common historical revolutions which reflect nationalistic struggles, and which aim at supporting nationalism.'[69]

Nationalistic or ethnic revolutionary movements are the strongest and most crucial of all social movements because they are often their source. 'Ethnic identity is', for Qadhdhafi, 'the fundamental basis of the continued existence of nations.'[70] It may be useful at this point, therefore, to analyze his views, as expressed in the official commentary on *The Green Book*, of *qawmiyah* (ethnic identity) and *umamiyah* (multi-ethnic nationalism or internationalism).

A *qawm* is a group of people, nation or group of nations sharing a common language, history and cultural heritage. The word '*qawmiyah*' was derived from '*qawm*' to mean nationalism as understood in the West. Both the term and concept, as they are now understood, are foreign to classical Arabic culture. This is not to say that Arabs before and after Islam were unaware of their identity and special place in the Muslim community. The terms of reference, however, were those of a classical society dominated by tribal and genealogical considerations. Even though ethnic, linguistic, historical and cultural factors have become the framework of contemporary nationalistic ideas, in the case of Arab identity ethnic and linguistic considerations take precedence. Historic factors have been expressed in terms of a common past and a future destiny.

The word '*ummah*' means a community of people sharing a common purpose, faith or destiny. The plural of *ummah* is *umam*, hence the noun *umamiyah*. *Umamiyah* as an ideology is considered by Qadhdhafi as a tool in the hands of capitalist imperialism in its bid to dominate the world. The commentary on *The Green Book* tells us that 'The thesis of internationalism [*umamiyah*] is, in all honesty, a kind of neo-imperialism.'[71] This is because this ideology does not respect the national, ethnic and geographical boundaries of others. It rests on the principle that 'might is right'. Thus those nations which have adopted this ideology have used it to usurp the wealth of other societies on the grounds that these societies are technologically unable to exploit their own natural resources, and hence should entrust them to those who are able to do so. The commentator on *The Green Book* goes so far as to reject the *umamiyah*, or concept of an international order, based solely on a common religious identity. Likewise, the new trend in which ethnic and religious groups advocate internationalism as a world identity will inevitably lead to "the destruction of civilizations and the annihilation of many social entities. It will lead to intense struggles, regardless of the thought content of this ideology, whether it be religious or non-religious"[72] Reference here is perhaps to contemporary pan-Islamic movements such as the Society of Muslim Brothers, about which more will be said later.

Qadhdhafi asserts that only those nations which lost their ethnic identities eventually vanished. At best, such bygone nations have continued to exist as oppressed minorities. Ethnic identity, and the loyalty it engenders, is like the force of gravity among heavenly bodies. When this force is lost, the galaxy, in this case of like ethnic groups, is destroyed. This is because 'the gravitational force cementing the social tie is the secret of the continued existence of society'.[73]

The only rival to this common social factor is, according to Qadhdhafi, the religious factor. Religion can divide an otherwise unified people, and is capable of uniting groups of diverse ethnic and cultural backgrounds. Yet in the end the social factor would prevail over the religious one. Qadhdhafi then concludes: 'To every people [*qawm*] their own religion.' 'This,' he asserts, 'is what the true harmony of human society requires. Yet this is often not the case in the history of many nations'.

In spite of his unquestionable faith and commitment to the spread of Islam throughout the world, Qadhdhafi follows his logic to its ultimate conclusion. He thus elaborates: 'The sound principle is that every people must have their own religion. The opposite is a deviation with unfortunate consequences. The obverse side of the principle has created an unhealthy reality which has been the cause of much dissension within societies of a single ethnic background.' The only solution, Qadhdhafi concludes, is 'adherence to his natural principle, which is "to every people their religion". Thus would concord between the religious and social factors be achieved, and harmony prevail. Then good order in the life of society would be established, allowing it to grow in a sound and healthy manner.'[74]

Among the strong links in society is marriage. Even though the man and woman must be free in their mutual acceptance of one another, this being a fundamental principle of human freedom, still marriage within a society with a common ethnic and religious background helps buttress its social growth and unity. The family is, therefore, more important for the individual than the state. A sane man knows that his family is his natural origin and environment; it is his social shelter.

Qadhdhafi is here speaking from the experience of an extended family, clan and even tribe. He compares the family to a plant, and the state, or ethnic society, to a garden nourishing many plants. The basic and natural element is the plant, while the garden is a necessary but artificial creation. Carrying this analogy further, Qadhdhafi concludes: 'Any situation, circumstance, or action that would lead to the disintegration or destruction of the family, is inhuman and unnatural. It is rather an arbitrary situation.'[75]

Next in importance to the family as a social unit is the tribe. Even though most modern societies are no longer tribal, Qadhdhafi believes the tribe to be one of the primary units of all societies. He writes: 'the tribe is a family which has grown as a result of procreation'. He goes on to assert further that the nation is in reality a tribe which has grown through the same process, and the world is likewise a large nation which has also grown and divided into many branches. Moreover, the same ties which link the family also link the tribe, the nation and even the world. These ties, however, become less effective in proportion to the increase of the number of families, tribes or nations. Qadhdhafi thus concludes: 'Humanity is actually ethnic identity, or nationalism. Nationalism is a form of tribalism, and tribalism is originally family ties. The strength of this tie, however, diminishes gradually from the smallest to the largest unit [of society].'[76]

Qadhdhafi regards the tribe as the healthiest unit of society. He observes that basic social values such as love and amity as well as other social ties tend to disappear among the nations of the world. They must be preserved if humanity is to achieve a 'good life' on earth. Among the benefits of the tribe, and one which the family lacks, is the conduct which it fosters among its members. It is a civic ethical code, better and more noble than any pedagogical code found in the schools or any other civic institutions of society. This is because all the members of a tribe are bound by a special code of conduct which is naturally designed to preserve its system of values. Tribal allegiance is based on blood relationship and custom. Thus the tribe provides a natural social security and defence for all the members, in a way that no other social structure can provide. The second benefit which the tribe provides is the psychological release mechanism through the honour system and vendetta. These tribal virtues apparently outweigh for Qadhdhafi all other considerations, such as those of the traditionalism and social stagnation which tribalism tends to reinforce.

The nation provides a wider social, political and ethnic environment than that of the tribe. Qadhdhafi then presents the reverse of the process of family, tribe and nation building. He asserts that family ties tend to weaken tribal allegiances, and these in turn tend to weaken national loyalties. Yet, however necessary fanatical nationalism may be for the strength and cohesion of the nation, it none the less becomes a threat to humanity. Qadhdhafi declares: 'Fanatical nationalism, the use of nationalist sentiment and force by one nation against a weak one, and the achievement of national prosperity by usurping the wealth of another nation, is evil and harmful to humanity.'[77]

Qadhdhafi extols those persons who have strength of character, self-confidence and a good sense of responsibility. Such a person is an asset to the family. A family whose members have these civic virtues is useful to the tribe, and a nation with such qualities is necessary for world harmony and peace. The social and political structure of any society deteriorates when it descends to the level of narrow tribal and family structures, interacts with them and acquires their characteristics.

Qadhdhafi presents a simple and traditional theory of the rise of nations. Nations are the children of time. The passing of time helps create new nations from families and tribes and destroys older ones. A common origin and a common destiny are the fundamental historical bases of a nation. Yet a nation is not based only on a common ethnic origin, even though ethnicity is necessary for its growth and continued existence. Qadhdhafi further argues that a nation is the result of the accumulation of historical and social circumstances which helps bring diverse groups of people together to share a particular heritage and a common destiny. 'Thus a nation is in the end, regardless of a common ancestry, a common affiliation and destiny.'[78]

Qadhdhafi observes that many great nations have appeared on the stage of history, and many have disappeared. He then asks whether the reason for this has always been simply political or social factors. His answer is that the political growth of a nation from a variety of ethnic groups will inevitably lead to disintegration, as each ethnic group would seek to preserve its own distinct ethnic identity, if necessary at the expense of national sovereignty. The existence of a nation rests on many factors. The simplest of these is ethnic identity. Yet an ethnic nation is the only political structure which can be integrated with its natural social structure. Such a nation would continue to grow in strength and solidarity as long as it was not challenged by a stronger ethnic identity, or as long as its political structure was subject to its society structure, as embodied in families, clans and tribes. Other important factors in the making of a nation are complex religious and economic issues. Yet in the end the social or ethnic factors prevail, even though this is always preceded by a temporary victory of the religious affiliation over the ethnic or social identity. If the political structure or ideology of a nation clashes with its ethnic or social identity, it will be doomed to failure.[79]

After this general theoretical framework, Mu'ammar al-Qadhdhafi takes up specific elements of society to illustrate his theory. He first deals with the character, rights and status of women in society. Here he is guided by the traditions of Islam as well as those of his own society. He begins with what he considers as self-evident truth – namely, that 'Woman and man are both human, without any doubt or disagreement. Thus women and men are equal in their humanity, and any distinction between them on the human plane is an act of naked and unjustifiable oppression.'[80] Their distinct physical differences, however, indicate that each has a distinct role to play in society which is dictated by these differences. A female menstruates, becomes pregnant and must nurse her child. These biological functions make her, during such times, ill or incapable of being a fully active member of society. They thus create in her basic physical traits, characteristics which are natural and not a result of choice. The alternative to these biological functions is the end of the human race. Thus both birth control and bottle-feeding are contrary to life, according to Qadhdhafi.

Qadhdhafi argues further that neglecting the woman's role as a mother and having her place taken by day-care centres deprives her of her human dignity and natural medium of self-expression. The mother and the home are the natural shelter for a child. Therefore, sending a child to a nursery is an act of coercion and oppression of the child. It is, in short, depriving the child of its natural freedom.

Qadhdhafi considers placing pregnant women in positions of physical exertion, such as factory work, mining and the like, as an arbitrary and unnatural situation. He considers this to be 'a tax which a woman must pay in order for her to enter the world of men'.[81] The belief that women undertake such physical tasks voluntarily is false. Rather, today's materialistic society has forced her into this role on the basis of the principle which states that 'There is no difference between man and woman in anything'. He objects: 'The phrase, "in anything" is the great deceiver of the woman'.[82] This is because this principle has prevented the woman from living a natural life and fulfilling her needs in accordance with her biological nature.

Qadhdhafi's view of women is essentially a traditional one. A woman must be feminine and beautiful. Thus any hard task requiring physical strength, or any dirty work which may distort her beauty, is an act of oppression.

Qadhdhafi argues that the notion that there is 'no difference between man and woman' only applies to their common humanity, their rights and freedom. It specifically means that neither should be forced to marry or divorce the other without their mutual agreement, or a just ruling by the authorities concerned.[83] The woman is free only when she is allowed to be a female – a female who must marry and procreate, and be both delicate and attractive. Because man is stronger by nature, his freedom lies in his exercise of strength and manliness. This is a law of nature which governs both the animal and plant kingdoms. Qadhdhafi predicts that a world revolution, which will end once and for all the social and economic circumstances which have forced women to do a man's work in order that they may have equal rights, is inevitable. 'This revolution shall certainly come, especially in industrialized societies, as an instinctive action of survival.'[84]

This revolution is necessary, however, in both the East and West. Indeed, it is necessary for world society. Qadhdhafi writes: 'All societies today look at the woman as a commodity. The East looks at her as a merchandise which can be bought and sold. The West looks at her not as a female.'[85] The question for Qadhdhafi is not whether women must work. Society must provide work for all its members, but each according to his or her ability and physical nature.

In 1983 the women's military academy of Tripoli graduated its first class. In Libya today polygamy is prohibited except in very special circumstances. Both of these measures go against traditional Islamic law. But Qadhdhafi has argued that both decisions reflect a truer and more proper understanding of Islam than that of the traditional jurists who deprived women of their natural rights and freedom.

The next category of oppressed people that Qadhdhafi treats are the minorities. He distinguishes two kinds of minorities: one which belongs to a national entity, which then becomes the framework for its existence, and another which has no national base. The latter has no social framework except its own social structure. This kind of minority is the result of a long accumulation of historical circumstances which have given rise to a feeling of solidarity and shared destiny. This minority must not be deprived of its social rights by the majority. The political dilemma of this minority can only be solved in a socialist society in which the masses exercise control over civic and political authority, wealth and arms. Qadhdhafi concludes, 'To consider a minority as a political and economic one [that is to deprive it of these rights] is dictatorship and oppression.'[86] The question of minorities has for Mu'ammar al-Qadhdhafi important religious as well as national implications, which will be discussed later.

On 1 September 1969, al-Qadhdhafi led not a simple *coup d'état* but a revolution. His aim was not to change a regime, or substitute one type of government for another, but to build a new society which would need no government. *The Green Book* is only one, albeit an important step, toward the fulfilment of this aim. This revolution was to change first Libyan society, then the Arab nation, and finally the world. An internal programme has been designed to develop and implement an Islamic philosophy of socialism. The natural ground wherein this philosophy is to be planted and bear fruit is a united, free and strong Arab nation. It is to be a nation free from both the capitalist and Marxist ideologies, free from their intellectual, economic and spiritual domination.

So far neither of these great dreams has been fulfilled. The Arab nation is still divided within and against itself. It is dominated by a large number of competing ideologies and foreign economic enterprises. Its rulers are still kings, some both in name and reality, and others in reality if not in name. Neither socialism nor Islam plays a decisive role in Arab society. Socialism, even in Libya, is not without its problems. More than a dozen years after the revolution, Qadhdhafi admitted that the Libyan people had not yet understood the Third Universal Theory, even though they live by it.[87] Yet Qadhdhafi goes on as tenaciously and vigorously with work to which he has dedicated himself as when he started as a dreaming agitator in secondary school.

In the end it will be not the Third Universal Theory in itself, but what it has achieved in the social, political and economic life of the people, which will speak for its success or failure. Qadhdhafi's vision is subject to the political, social and economic vicissitudes of politics and history. His Islamic faith has, on the other hand, already withstood the test of time and is shared by millions of men and women who, like him, find in it the meaning and fulfilment of their lives and history. It is the elements of his faith, ultimately the impetus for Qadhdhafi's political concerns, to which we now turn.

Notes

1 See Omar I. El Fathaly and Monte Palmer, *Political Development and Social Change in Libya* (Lexington, Mass., Lexington Books, 1969) pp. 15–20.

2 *Ibid.*, pp. 20–3.

3 *Ibid.*, pp. 26–7.

4 *Ibid.*, p. 40.

5 See Chapter 1 above, p. 21.

6 Ahmad 'Abd al-Hamid al-Khalidi, *Usus al-Tanzim al-Sisayi fi al-Nazariyah al-'Alamiyah al-Thalithah* (Tripoli, al-Munsha'ah al-Ammah lil-Nashr wa-al-Tawzi' wa-al-I'lan, 1983), pp. 267–8.

7 Jamal 'Abd al-Nasser, *Falsafat al-Thawrah wa-al-Mithaq*, 1st edn. (Beirut, Dar al-Qalam, 1970), pp. 84–90.

8 See below in this chapter.

9 See al-Khalidi, *Usus al-Tanzim*, pp. 273–5.

10 *Ibid.*, p. 277.

11 *Ibid.*, p. 278.

12 *Ibid.*, pp. 283–91.

13 *Ibid.*, pp. 291–4.

14 *Ibid.*, p. 299.

15 *al-Sijill al-Qawmi*, vol. 1, 1969–70, p. 234. See also Qadhdhafi's later and equally emphatic rejection of political parties in the speech he delivered on the occasion of the Prophet's birthday in the city of Zwarah, 15 April 1973, in *ibid.*, vol. 4 (1972–73) pp. 505–6.

16 *Ibid.*, vol. 4, pp. 501ff. See also Sami G. Hajjar, 'The Jamahiriya experiment in Libya: Gadhafi and Rousseau', in *The Journal of Modern African Studies*, 18, 2 (1980), 182ff.

17 *al-Sijill al-Qawmi*, vol. 4, pp. 504–4.
18 *Ibid.*, pp. 785–6.
19 *'Al-Qur'an shari'at-al-mujtama''* ('The Qur'an is the sacred law of society'), one of the important slogans of the revolution. See Chapter 3 below, 'The Law of Society: the Qur'an and Prophetic Tradition'.
20 *al-Sijill al-Qawmi*, vol. 8 (1976–77), pp. 471ff.
21 See Chapter 1 above.
22 *al-Sijill al-Qawmi*, vol. 7 (1975–76), p. 1093.
23 Qur'an 42:38.
24 *al-Kitab al-Akhdar* (*The Green Book*), Tripoli, al-Markaz al-'Alami li-Dirasat wa-Abhath al-Kitab al-Akhdar, n.d.) part 1, p. 6.
25 *al-Sijill al-Qawmi*, vol. 8, p. 610.
26 See *al-Kitab al-Akhdar*, part 1, p. 1.
27 *Ibid.*, pp. 25ff. See also *al-Sijill al-Qawmi*, vol. 14 (1982–3), pp. 610–11.
28 *al-Kitab al-Akhdar*, p. 30.
29 *Ibid.*, p. 34.
30 *Ibid.*, p. 35. See also pp. 33–4.
31 *Ibid.*, p. 39.
32 *Ibid.*, p. 39.
33 *Ibid.*, p. 45.
34 *Ibid.*, p. 45.
35 *Christian Science Monitor*, 7 April 1977, p. 7.
36 'Ali al-Siddiq al-Madani, *al-Ta'rif bi-al-Nizam al-Jamahiri* (Tripoli, Manshurat al-Markaz al-'Alami li-Dirasat wa-Abhath al-Kitab al-Akhdar, n.d.), pp. 15–16.
37 See al-Khalidi, pp. 345ff.
38 *al-Kitab al-Akhdar*, part 1, pp. 48–9.
39 Qur'an 30:30.
40 *al-Sijill al-Qawmi*, vol. 7 (1975–76), p. 484.
41 *al-Kitab al-Akhdar*, part 1, p. 59.
42 *Ibid.*, p. 57.
43 *al-Sijill al-Qawmi*, vol. 7, pp. 485–6.
44 *al-Kitab al-Akhdar*, part 1, pp. 55–6.
45 *Ibid.*, p. 63.
46 *Ibid.*, p. 70.
47 *Ibid.*, p. 71.
48 Anon. (Qadhdhafi?), *Shuruh al-Kitab al-Akhdar*, 1–2 vols. (Tripoli, al-Markaz al-'Alami li-Dirasat wa-Abhath al-Kitab al-Akhdar, 1983), vol. 1, p. 8.
49 *Ibid.*, pp. 16–17.
50 *Ibid.*, p. 26.
51 *al-Kitab al-Akhdar*, part 2, p. 78.
52 *Ibid.*, pp. 80–1.
53 *Ibid.*, p. 82.

54 *Ibid.*, p. 90.
55 *Ibid.*, p. 90.
56 *Ibid.*, p. 91.
57 *Ibid.*, pp. 91–2.
58 *Ibid.*, p. 92.
59 *Ibid.*, pp. 92–3.
60 *Ibid.*, p. 95.
61 *Ibid.*, pp. 96–7.
62 *Ibid.*, pp. 103–4.
63 *Ibid.*, p. 105.
64 *Ibid.*, p. 110.
65 *Ibid.*, p. 110.
66 *Ibid.*, p. 112.
67 *Ibid.*, p. 117.
68 *Ibid.*, p. 119.
69 *Ibid.*, p. 120.
70 *Ibid.*, p. 121.
71 *Shuruh al-Kitab al-Akhdar*, vol. 1, p. 148.
72 *Ibid.*, p. 149.
73 *al-Kitab al-Akhdar*, part 3, pp. 122–3.
74 *Ibid.*, pp. 123–4.
75 *Ibid.*, p. 128.
76 *Ibid.*, pp. 130–1.
77 *Ibid.*, p. 136.
78 *Ibid.*, p. 137.
79 *Ibid.*, pp. 137–44.
80 *Ibid.*, p. 147.
81 *Ibid.*, p. 157.
82 *Ibid.*, p. 158.
83 Ann Mayer, 'Developments in the Law of Marriage and Divorce in Libya since the 1969 Revolution', in *Journal of African Law*, 22, no. 1, pp. 30–49.
84 *al-Kitab al-Akhdar*, part 3, p. 164.
85 *Ibid.*, p. 164. See also pp. 173–4.
86 *al-Kitab al-Akhdar*, part 3, p. 174.

3
Qadhdhafi's Faith

Religious faith consists of three essential dimensions: commitment, praxis and philosophy. These three dimensions, however, are not separate or independent operations of faith. Rather, they are aspects of one reality, and no one can exist without the others. When commitment is a mere formal and tepid identity, or when it is compromised, then it is *shirk*, or association of other beings or things in the worship of God. When it is blind, uncompromising and exclusivistic, then it is *nifaq*, or hypocrisy. Thus only when commitment is a sincere acceptance of faith in God as the one Eternal Sovereign Lord, Merciful Creator and Sustainer of His creation, can it be the basis of meaningful praxis and sound philosophy. Praxis would then be a true manifestation of the commitment of faith in worship and 'good works'. A philosophy of faith is a process of understanding and interiorization of commitment and worship which begins with birth and ends when the reality of faith is seen 'not through a glass darkly', but face to face, when the people of faith shall, with 'radiant faces, gaze upon their Lord'.[1] It is with these essential dimensions of Mu'ammar al-Qadhdhafi's faith that we shall be concerned in this and the following chapters.

Qadhdhafi's commitment to the Islamic faith is evident. He has been known to interrupt meetings with heads of state and other important international dignitaries so that he could offer his prayers at their proper times. He has often presented committed atheists – leaders of the Soviet Union and those of other countries of the communist block – with copies of the Qur'an, earning by this a reputation as a preacher of Islam in high places. Commitment to Islamic worship, moral imperatives and legal injunctions is an integral part of his personality and upbringing, as it is indeed of that of the majority of his compatriots. This has been well illustrated in the first chapter of this study and may be dramatically seen again in the following anecdote.

In the last days before the start of the revolution of 1 September, Colonel Qadhdhafi with a few of his fellow officers was travelling at high speed at night. They carried with them, in a private car belonging to one of the young officers, a wine bottle filled with distilled water. The car overturned, and local peasants gathered at the scene of the accident to offer their help. One of the men saw the bottle and, suspecting the accident to have been the result of drunken driving, began to mutter: 'I seek refuge in God from the accursed Satan.' Qadhdhafi observed later in his memoirs: 'We were not then in a position that would have allowed us to defend ourselves so that we could assure him that we too hate alcohol as much as he does, and even more, and that we would ban it after the Revolution.'[2]

Tripoli before the revolution was the 'fun city' of North Africa. After the revolution, however, not only was alcohol banned, but all forms of frivolous and permissive entertainment were also outlawed. Indeed, one of the reasons for the radical change which the revolution brought about was the corruption and immorality which dominated Libyan cities before the revolution. Although our main concern in this study is with Qadhdhafi's words and thoughts rather than actions, it must none the less be observed that one of the earliest decisions of the Revolutionary Command Council was to establish a society for the propagation of Islam, the Islamic Call Society, which has been active in numerous educational and humanitarian endeavours in many countries of Asia, Africa, Europe and North and South America.

Islam and the Universality of Faith

Qadhdhafi sees a basic human need for a religious faith and order. In the modern world, this need stems from the materialism and immorality which characterize contemporary society, and especially that of the industrialized and affluent countries of the world. Any materialistic civilization which does not possess a religious faith and a spiritual heritage capable of leading its people to the worship of God, would be like that of *'Ad* and *Thamud* in the Qur'an[3] which God destroyed because of their corruption.[4] Islam is, for Qadhdhafi, the only religious faith capable of restoring that balance which God willed for human beings between material concerns and the moral and spiritual quest.

In the first conference of the Islamic Call Society, held in Tripoli in December 1970, Qadhdhafi set forth his views on Islam with characteristic confidence and directness. Islam, he asserted, is the last divine address to humanity, and Muhammad is the seal of God's messengers to humankind. It is, therefore, the responsibility of every Muslim to spread this universal faith, and to strive in its cause, so that the 'word of God remains uppermost'[5] till the Day of Resurrection. Islam was not meant for one specific tribe, a specific area of the world, or a limited period of time. Rather, because it is the last religion, it is meant for all peoples, times and places. 'This religion has certain characteristics which make it capable of being spread in all areas of the world, if Muslims were to strive steadfastly towards achieving this goal.'[6] Islam, Qadhdhafi believes, is not understood in the West, and is thus wrongly portrayed as a reactionary religion. This misconception is due to the fact that Muslims have themselves often reduced Islamic rituals to superstition and a kind of magical practice.

Qadhdhafi holds the traditional view that all branches of knowledge, moral principles and human aspirations have their basis in the Qur'an. Thus, for instance, sciences such as mathematics and astronomy are said to be referred to in the Qur'an in verses which discuss the phases of the moon and the reckoning of months and years.[7] Likewise, Qadhdhafi sees that the ideal of liberty for which humankind is ever yearning is set forth in the Qur'an, 'and that its foundations have been firmly established by Islam.[8]

As will be made amply clear throughout this discussion, Qadhdhafi has consistently called for new interpretations and applications of Islamic principles. Like many Muslim thinkers before him, he has argued for returning to the Qur'an, and the Qur'an alone, for guidance. This of course requires that the Qur'an be interpreted anew if Muslims are to apply its broad principles of moral uprightness, equality, freedom and social justice to their lives. Were this process of Qur'anic interpretation to be seriously undertaken, Qadhdhafi believes,

the enemies of Islam would find that the essence of this
religion is more progressive than communism – if indeed,
communism can claim to be progressive. It is more capable

than communism, which despises all religions, of establishing a sound and just economic social order and more capable than it of ensuring happiness, prosperity and freedom for all human societies. Long before communist thinkers called for social reform, the Qur'an demanded of its adherents that they stand by the poor and struggling classes of society. This challenge was first presented by God to the Prophet of Islam himself when he was reproached by Him in the Qur'an for making the error of preferring the powerful men of Quraysh to a poor and helpless blind man, even though he had done so only in order to win the men of Quraysh to Islam.[9]

Mu'mmar al-Qadhdhafi is not a trained Islamic thinker. He is rather a concerned and sometimes impatient Muslim revolutionary. His concern, like that of many Muslim social and political activists, is to make the Islamic heritage of a thousand years ago relevant to today's problems. This concern may be clearly discerned in the answer to a question which a member of the Department of Justice in Tripoli posed concerning the application of the *Shari'ah* law in Libya after the revolution. The question was asked in April 1971, before the appearance of *The Green Book* and the crystallization of the Third Universal Theory. Thus both the question and Qadhdhafi's answer reflect the formative period of the revolution of 1 September. Qadhdhafi said: 'By the *shari'ah* I mean the Religion which will endure till the Day of Resurrection. God revealed many principles and precepts concerning it. The Qur'an does not limit itself to the general problems of everyday life, but rather enters into specific details. For God says, "We have not neglected anything in this Book".[10] What we must not allow to happen is narrow mindedness.' This is because, he continued, narrow mindedness only strengthens those who are in reality opposed to the *shari'ah*. What is needed is positive change, or progress. By change, however, is not meant altering the basic principles, or essence of the faith or *shari'ah*, but change in the ways in which they can be applied to today's conditions and problems.[11]

Islam is, for Qadhdhafi, a universal religion not only because it can speak to the conditions of human beings in every age, but also because it is universal in its capacity to explain all the phenomena of nature and of human society. It is for him a unique and coherent divine message communicated by God to humanity through the

Prophet Muhammad in the Qur'an. Thus in an interview with the German magazine *Der Spiegel*, held in January 1972, Qadhdhafi declared: 'Islam is a universal religion which explains the universe and the meaning of life. All the problems which we have been discussing are particulars whose general roots are in Islam. Do not look at Islam as a sect, or particular school of religious thought [*madhhab*]. Rather look at it as a universal religion which explains the phenomena of the universe and life, as well as the life of its community at the same time.'[12]

Qadhdhafi has advocated a flexible approach to Islam. Such an approach would seek to implement not only the *shari'ah*, wherever possible, but the spirit of the Qur'an and *sunnah* of the Prophet. In an interview in 1972 with *Qarinah*, a literary magazine published by the Faculty of Literature of the University of Qar Yunus, Benghazi, he was asked: 'In accordance with the resolution [recently passed by the government] concerning the promulgation of Islamic laws, can we say that our constitution now is the noble Qur'an and Prophetic *sunnah*, and could this be made public, and be implemented?' The Colonel answered: 'If we wish to implement the Islamic *shari'ah*, then relevant texts should be already in place. This, however, does not prevent the existence of other laws, just as the Prophet allowed in Medinah. Even though he already had Qur'anic texts and in spite of the fact that he continued to receive revelations, still he issued an edict resembling a constitution or a constitutional manifesto in which he set forth the various pacts and agreements with the Jewish community, and in which he elucidated the rights pertaining to the *dhimmah* [or pact between the Muslims and the people of the Book].' There is no reason why Libya could not do the same, Qadhdhafi declared: 'The important thing is that human rights and dignity must be safeguarded.'[13]

It should be observed that this open-ended approach to the *shari'ah* is neither a novelty nor what has been called in Islam 'reprehensible innovation' (*bid'ah*). Muslim rulers, jurists and ordinary men and women, following the death of the Prophet, had to find ways to interiorize and implement the moral and legal precepts of the Qur'an and Prophetic Tradition. Yet even though the Companions of the Prophet and their immediate Successors could be guided by their life experience in the community of Madinah, still disagreements eventually led to dissensions and schisms in the Muslim community, some of which have survived to this day. With wisdom and sincerity, this approach can be a dynamic and creative force in the life of the Islamic community (*ummah*), but it has not been so without some danger to the *shari'ah*, the formal law of Islam.

Qadhdhafi's attitude towards Islam is one as well of confident pride in a glorious heritage. This is an attitude shared by the vast majority of Muslims, an attitude which has sustained Muslim countries in times of humiliating defeat and colonization at the hands of Western powers. Often this attitude, evoked by the long history of conflict with the West, has in turn provoked a sharp reaction to all things Western: a permissive life style, and even Western science, education and high culture. This reaction is well illustrated in the remarks which Qadhdhafi made at a press conference held in Tripoli in March 1972. Asked to comment on a government decision to ban magazines with cover pictures of naked women, he retorted: 'An Arab citizen does not wish to be nurtured on empty notions or frivolous pictures. An Arab citizen wants a press which sheds light on his bitter reality, and points the way for him to a brighter future.' He made it clear that he regarded such pictures as no more than temptations for people to buy the magazines which carry them, and as an insult and a contradiction to the revolutionary Islamic values of the revolution of 1 September.[14]

Islam for Qadhdhafi is a perpetual revolution against unnecessary and illegitimate wealth, exploitation and oppression. For him as for revolutionaries everywhere from the time of at least the French Revolution, monarchical rule in particular is synonymous with oppression and injustice. Thus on another occasion he asserted that 'the Islam which both the East and the West knew was that observed by kings and princes, as well as mendicants [*darawish*] who live off Islam. Thus people thought of Islam as a reactionary movement, a message which could never keep up with life. They considered Islam simply as a religious heritage which could be venerated, but which had to be kept distant from the fields of action and human struggle.' Qadhdhafi sees Islam also as a call to universal brotherhood, or internationalism (*umamiyah*), as a real power which can move men and revitalize their energies: 'Without faith, man becomes a slave of the machine. But we Muslims are slaves of no one but God alone. We say openly that Islam is a call to progress, and that any other system such as communism or liberalism is a call to reactionism.'[15]

Mu'ammar Qadhdhafi affirms that Islam is the Divine message of truth. The Third Universal Theory is no more than a modern

restatement of this truth. It is not a new message, 'because there is
no new message after the message of the apostle Muhammad'. He
goes on: 'As we are now in the thick of the struggle, it is imperative
for us to clarify our distinctive personality, our national identity and
the way of truth which we follow. For any man who follows a way
other than the truth will not reach his goal, but will surely go
astray.'[16]

Libya, like other countries of North Africa, is a traditional
country with an essentially desert society. It is far less touched by
Western values than its neighbours. Thus what the West considers
as an austere life style is often the normal way of life for many
traditional Muslim societies. In an interview in December 1972 with
an Italian journalist, it was suggested to Qadhdhafi that under the
influence of the Islamic *shari'ah* Libyan society is forced to endure
unnatural austerities. Qadhdhafi remarked angrily: 'I deny that
there is a situation of austerity in Libya, unless you mean by
austerity the lack of places where women can be bought and sold,
and where there are no taverns! If this is what you think, then such
ideas would have to be rejected by any reasonable, thinking
person.'[17] A simple and somewhat austere way of life has its basis
both in social tradition and Islamic morality. Qadhdhafi believes
that moral living is based on the belief in man's accountability
before God on the Day of Judgement. 'Why are we bound by a
moral system?' he asks. 'It is', he answers, 'because we shall be held
accountable for our actions.' He then quoted the Qur'anic verse:
'Whoever does an atom's weight of good shall see it, and whoever
does an atom's weight of evil shall see it.'[18]

The Green Book, as we saw in the last chapter, insists that the
sound principle on which the structure of any society must rest is 'To
every people their own religion'. The reality, however, as *The
Green Book* further insists, is the reverse of this principle.[19] Yet
religion plays as significant a role in human history as nationalism.
Thus Qadhdhafi holds the view that religion and nationalism are the
two prime movers of human history.[20] A way must, therefore, be
found to minimize the social discord resulting from the possible
clash between religious and national identity, at least within
societies of similar ethnic backgrounds. Qadhdhafi presents two
different but closely related solutions to this problem. The first is an
Islamic solution, and the second is what may be called the trans-
cedent unity of all religions, or at least of the three monotheistic
faiths: Judaism, Christianity and Islam.

During a visit to Sri Lanka in August 1976, Qadhdhafi addressed the Muslims of that highly pluralistic country and counselled them to coexist peacefully with people of other faiths. He also urged them to show loyalty to their nation. This, he pointed out, is necessary because Islam is a universal message of peace, as the Islamic greeting 'Peace be upon you' clearly shows. He further argued, 'Since the motto of Muslims is peace, then they must be missionaries of peace everywhere.'[21] At the same time, he did not reject the need for propagation of Islam: Islam is, after all, a proselytizing religion. His idea is that Muslims must convey the message of Islam to all people. This is the true and continuous *jihad*, or struggle in the way of God. Islam cannot, Qadhdhafi asserted, be spread by force, but by persuasion. He concluded: 'We feel that the whole world is now in need of the Islamic faith. This is because all other religions have become incapable of solving the spiritual problems of humankind. Islam is therefore the only religion capable of offering the final solution to humanity's problems.'[22]

The universal appeal of Islam may be seen in the cultural, racial and linguistic breadth and variety of the Muslim world. Islam is both Eastern and Western, an Asian, African, European and American religion. There is no doubt that Qadhdhafi's vision of Islam is based on this phenomenon. Yet because of Islam's universal character, it presents a real challenge to any nationalistic movement or ideology. Qadhdhafi recognized this in his opening address to the eighth conference of the foreign ministers of the Muslim world on 13 May 1977. He began by asserting that the Prophet Muhammad was entrusted by God with the final revelation to humankind, a revelation which made all men equal before God, regardless of their national identities, colours and languages. He noted that the meeting of so many people representing so many different languages, races and cultures under the banner of Islam was eloquent testimony to the universality and internationalism of Islam. 'Islam was the seal of the revelations from God', Qadhdhafi asserted, 'because all the religions which came before it were local dispensations. They were concluded with Islam which is addressed to all humanity.'[23]

Earlier it was observed that an important part of Qadhdhafi's religious faith is his concern for the welfare of human beings. We also observed his aversion to fanaticism and narrow mindedness, whether practised by Muslims or any other religious community. In this spirit he praised the Red Cross for its humanitarian work and called for the strengthening of the Red Crescent, so that 'the cross and the crescent may work side by side in the world'. He even spoke approvingly of Christian missionary organizations spreading the Christian faith in the world. 'It is a great thing that they are preaching religion.' But he wished that American money was not behind such noble endeavours. He finally called for the establishment of a special Islamic international fund for the purpose of spreading Islam. 'Yet we do not wish', he insisted, 'to turn Christians into Muslims. There are, however, millions of people in the world who are either without faith at all, or who adhere to natural religions. We should seek first to; turn these millions of people to religion; then all will be easy.'[24]

So far Qadhdhafi has been speaking about institutionalized Islam, the Islam of the Muslim community. This institutionalized Islam is a universal and comprehensive system of religious, social, political and economic values. As such, it alone is capable of solving the moral, social and spiritual problems of humanity. Yet this system is only the temporal manifestation of a primordial and eternal Islam. It is an 'Islam divinely conceived; it is more universal than the message revealed to, and delivered by, our master Muhammad.' This Islam goes back to the Prophet Abraham, the father of prophets and first true Muslim. Qadhdhafi cites the Qur'anic verse: 'It is the religion [*millah*] of your father Abraham; it is he who called you Muslims aforetime',[25] then comments, 'Islam is therefore ancient, going back to the time of Abraham, and even to the beginning of creation. "The seal of the prophets" [Muhammad] came only to conclude all Divine messages with Islam.'[26]

What is this 'primordial and eternal Islam'? It is, even though Qadhdhafi does not say so in so many words, an Islam without *shari'ah*. 'Islam', he says, 'is that we all submit peacefully to the will of God, exalted be He, whatever our races and colors may be. [Islam] is to worship the One and only God. It is to perform good deeds and to believe in God, his messengers and his angels.'[27] With the coming of Muhammad, Islam was given its final character and framework. Hence, Qadhdhafi argues, after Muhammad there are no longer Muslims and non-Muslims. Rather all those who believe in God and do good, regardless of what specific religion they adhere to, are Muslims in the broadest possible meaning of this word. He thus concludes: 'I believe that all problems would be solved within the framework of the "Divine conception", within the framework of this reality. If we all were to believe in the One God and do good, the problem would be finished. It would then not matter to me whether you follow Muhammad, Jesus or Moses.'[28]

Nowhere has religion played such a crucial, and often divisive, role in human history as in the Middle East. It has been the cause of war and disunity, and often provided the framework for co-operation and peaceful coexistence among peoples of diverse racial, linguistic and cultural backgrounds. Most significantly, however, from Colonel Qadhdhafi's point of view, religion has been an obstacle in the way of achieving Arab unity in the modern world. Thus the essential purpose behind his appeal for religious concord is the restoration of national unity among the Arabs. It is only a united Arab nation, stretching from the Gulf to the Atlantic, Qadhdhafi believes, which would be able to face the pressures of world imperialism and assume a leadership role in the Muslim community at large and the Third World. He is not calling for a secular society without a religious faith, but for a society guided by the moral and spiritual values of its religious heritage. We shall return to this important point in the following chapter; suffice it here to say that for Qadhdhafi it is Islam in its broadest sense as a universal religion and civilization to which the Arabs belong, whether they are Muslims, Jews or Christians, a universal religion which must be recognized by all men. Sectarian differences among both Muslims and Christians have played a negative role in the history of the two communities, and must therefore be eliminated. There is, in Qadhdhafi's view, no justification for anyone to stir up conflict among Muslims and Christians and to claim by this to be defending either Islam or Christianity.

Qadhdhafi returns to the theme of the Divine conception of Islam to argue on the basis of the Qur'an that all the prophets were in reality Muslims, and that each one of them had enjoined his people to submit themselves to God.[29] He admits that true submission to universal Islam was not realized even in the time of the Prophet Muhammad. The Qur'an reports that both the Jews and Christians of the Prophet's time claimed guidance and truth to be in their religion alone: 'They said, "Be Jews or Christians in order that you may be guided." "Rather", the Prophet was told to retort, "[we follow] the religion of Abraham, a man of pure faith, nor was he one of the Associators [of other things with God]." '[30]

Islam is faith in and submission to the One God. But because God is one, so also is true faith. Muslims should not be simply followers of Muhammad, but must believe in all the messengers and prophets. In support of this assertion, Qadhdhafi again quotes the words of the Qur'an: 'Say, "We believe in that which was sent down to us and that which was sent down to you. Our God and your God is one God, and to Him we have submitted." '[31] In accordance with this verse, Qadhdhafi has argued that the concept of Islam applies to all the messages of Divine Oneness. He says, 'The criterion is Divine Oneness and submission to God. Were we to follow this Divine conception of Islam, we would rise above our contemporary religions because we would find ourselves praying in one single rank before God.'[32] Qadhdhafi believes that Islam according to this Divine conception is not the Islam which Muslims today recognize and accept. According to the original Qur'anic view, this essential '*islam*', literally 'submission to God', was the faith of all the prophets and their true followers. Thus true Jews and Christians are also true Muslims.

> This means that the first revelation which came down from heaven to earth was intended to call people to this *islam*. It was necessary, moreover, that God should conclude His revelations with Islam, just as He opened them with it. It is also necessary that Islam alone should be manifested in order that whoever believes in the apostleship of our master Muhammad would have also believed in all the messengers who came before him, as well as the scriptures which were revealed before him. Thus would the Divine message to humankind be perfected.

This message is for all men; it is to worship together the One and only God. Any other belief or conception is an act of associating others in the worship of God.

Qadhdhafi thus counsels the men and women of the present time to reconsider their understanding of their own faith and the Divine revelation on which it is based, in light of these truths.[33]

This call for Christians and Jews to return to their own scriptures and judge by them is clearly stated in the Qur'an itself: 'Let the people of the Gospel judge in accordance with that which God has sent down in it. Whosoever does not judge in accordance with that which God has sent down – such are the unrighteous.'[34] The Qur'an reprimands the People of the Book – Jews and Christians – for altering or distorting the meaning of their scriptures. These general criticisms have led to the controversial theory in Islam of *tahrif* (distortion or alteration) by the Jews and Christians of their scriptures.[35] It must be noted that neither the Qur'an nor Prophetic Tradition provides a clear criterion for judgement as to the extent and nature of such wilful alteration. The only clear case is the references to Muhammad both in the Torah and the Gospel, which Jews are said to have either ignored or suppressed.[36] Qadhdhafi also insists that the recensions of both the Jewish Torah and the Christian Gospels do not represent the true revelations which God sent down to Moses and Jesus.

In February 1976, a Libyan-sponsored Muslim-Christian dialogue was held in Tripoli. In that meeting Qadhdhafi again called for better understanding and cooperation among the people of Divine scriptures: Jews, Christians and Muslims. 'Had the Muslims known the Qur'an truly, there would have been no essential disagreements which could lead to wars among them.' Yet the way Qadhdhafi saw the problem which has so far prevented the establishment of a true brotherhood of faith among the three Abrahamic communities, is itself a problem which might prevent any meaningful dialogue. He said, 'The problem is that until today Muslims have not returned to the Qur'an as they should, nor have the Christians and Jews returned to the true, or authentic [*sahih*] Torah and Gospel. It is this which has created conflicts among the people of faith.' This of course means that, in Qadhdhafi's view, the Qur'an is true and it is only Muslims who are in error, while both the scriptures of the Jews and Christians and they themselves are in error. In the end, Jews and Christians can recover the authenticity of their scriptures, and hence their faith, only by turning to the Qur'an, which Qadhdhafi has argued, '. . . could be a fundamental source for them both'.[37]

It must, however, be observed that Qadhdhafi's main purpose in promoting dialogue among people of faith is to promote harmony and cooperation among them. He is a religious man, and thus sees himself as having a common cause with religious Jews and Christians in striving against atheism and moral depravity among the young of the three communities. 'It is imperative that conflicts among us should cease as much as this is possible,' he pleads. 'We must overcome our problems in order that we do not promote atheism among our people and prevent them from abandoning faith altogether.'[38]

Qadhdhafi is not alone in his critique of the Jewish and Christian scriptures. In fact his critique essentially goes back to the rise of Islam. Yet while Muslims may, on doctrinal grounds, question the authenticity of the Gospel, they are in fact obliged by the Qur'an to accept and venerate all the prophets of God from Adam to Muhammad. Jews and Christians have, however, been unable to recognize Muhammad as a messenger of God and consequently they have not been able to accept the Qur'an as a divine revelation, not even in principle. At the same time Qadhdhafi has insisted that to deny the prophethood of Muhammad is to sin against God himself, because He spoke of his coming in all the scriptures previous to the Qur'an. Thus the most serious distortions by the Jews and the Christians of their own scriptures have been, in Qadhdhafi's view, the deletion of verses announcing the coming of Muhammad, or presenting the signs of his prophethood.[39]

The political implications of Colonel Qadhdhafi's views of other faiths are obvious. He is anxious to preserve and strengthen Arab unity across the religious differences between Muslims and Christians, as well as the sectarian differences within each of the two communities. He is also committed to the support of revolutionary movements regardless of the religious identity of the people involved. We shall return to these issues below, but one important point deserves some attention here.

In the Muslim-Christian dialogue meeting at Tripoli, Qadhdhafi observed that some Muslims believe that the war between Muslims and Christians, or between Muslims and Jews, is a holy war. This, he asserted was a mistaken view. 'This is because *jihad*, or armed struggle, must always be between the people of faith and the rejecters of faith. But between two groups of believers there is nothing called *jihad*. Rather it is warfare [*qital*].' The Qur'an, he went on, 'enjoins us to have dialogue with the people of the book as our people, since we and they are *muslims* to God'.[40]

In May 1978, Roger Garaudy, the well-known French intellectual, who had formerly been a Marxist and who subsequently accepted Islam, visited Mu'ammar al-Qadhdhafi in Libya. As they sat and talked under the desert sun, Qadhdhafi spoke of the necessity of *jihad* against the state of Israel. He declared, however, that 'It is impossible to have a war between Muslims and Christians, or between Muslims and Jews. This is because we all are the children of Abraham, our forefather. Furthermore, in our struggle against all kinds of idolatry, we and they are together, as we are all People of the Book.' The conflict with Israel, he stated, is strictly a political conflict. The issue is the illegal occupation of land, and the deprivation of the Palestinians of their legitimate rights. This conflict, however, has no religious overtones. Qadhdhafi continued: 'Any kind of religious fanaticism is a crime. All that we wish is amity and brotherhood among all the descendants of Abraham.'[41] He has, however, consistently called for *jihad* to liberate Palestine and particularly the holy city of Jerusalem from Zionist occupation, and has considered this goal as the duty of every Arab and every Muslim.

Relations between the Muslim community and both the Jewish and Christian communities have been at best ambivalent. All three communities share essentially a common religious faith and system of moral and social values. But it is their claims to an area of land, holy to all three faiths, their national aspirations and the long history of wars, conflict and colonialism which has dominated Muslim-Christian relations which has pulled them far apart. Like most Muslims and many Third World people, Qadhdhafi deplores this history which, in his view, is forever repeating itself. In the same speech in which Qadhdhafi argues that there cannot be a holy war between Muslims and the People of the Book, he speaks with reluctance and dismay of the Jewish-Christian alliance against the Muslims. He considers this alliance between Israel and the Christians of Lebanon and alliance of the former with America as in fact a kind of neo-crusade against Islam and Muslims.[42]

Qadhdhafi is avowedly guided by the Qur'an in both his national and international relations, and the Qur'an vividly reflects the long history of tense relations between the Muslim world and the People of the Book. The Qur'an for that reason invites the People of the Book 'to a word of common agreement' and purpose between them and the Muslims.[43] It commends the Christians for their tenderness and amity towards the Muslims, and for their recognition of truth.[44] It acknowledges with approbation those 'of the community of Moses who judge by the truth, and through it dispense justice'.[45] Yet the Qur'an also counsels the people of faith 'not to take the Jews and Christians as allies, for they are allies of one another. Whoever of you befriends them, shall be one of them.'[46] It is then to Qadhdhafi's view of the Qur'an and the place it occupies in his thought that we must now turn.

The Law of Society: the Qur'an and Prophetic Tradition

We saw in the last chapter that the 'natural law of society' must be based on an unchanging and inviolable source. *The Green Book* says, 'That a committee or assembly be appointed to promulgate the law of society: this is wrong and undemocratic! That the law of society be abolished or modified by an individual, committee, or assembly: this is also wrong and undemocratic.'[47] This 'unchanging and inviolable source' for the Muslim society is the Qur'an, the Book of God: 'Falsehood does not approach it, neither from before it nor from behind it.'[48] In the Qur'an, Qadhdhafi has sought the basis for his vision, his faith and his ideology. In it he has found the basis for his Islamic socialism and his nationalism, justification for his departure from tradition, and even for questioning the validity of the *hadith* as an equal or supplementary source of law with the Qur'an.

Mu'ammar al-Qadhdhafi defined the law of society, from an Islamic point of view, in the 'first intellectual gathering' of Arab students studying in Libya, held in Tripoli on 15–18 March 1982. One of the participants asked: 'What is the law of society? What is its main source, and of what benefit is it, from the democratic view point?' In answer to these questions Colonel Qadhdhafi gave the following concise definition:

(1) The law of society is a body of laws, general rules, sanctions and social customs which govern the progress of society towards the attainment of a comfortable life free from oppression and tyranny. [A just] society safeguards the rights of the individual, but without violating the rights of others, or neglecting the rights of God.

(2) The primary source of the law of society is the noble Qur'an, where God says, 'Surely this Qur'an guides to that which is most upright'.[49] The second source is the *sunnah* (life-example) of the Messenger of God. 'The *sunnah* came to confirm that which was revealed in the Qur'an. It is either [the *sunnah*] of speech, that is the *hadith* traditions which are reported from the Prophet, or [the *sunnah*] of action, that is the way the Messenger lived his actual daily life.'

(3) The third source is *qiyas* (analogical reasoning). It is the process of analogically deducing the solution to a problem concerning which no verse of the Qur'an was sent down, or

concerning which the *sunnah* has nothing to say.

(4) The fourth and final source is *ijtihad*, or the process of individual independent reasoning, and the use of scientific knowledge in arriving at religious and social laws and theories.[50]

As an example of his own *ijtihad*, Colonel Qadhdhafi gave a brief summary of the points dealing with the law of society in the first part of *The Green Book*. Even though *The Green Book* does not purport to offer an Islamic solution to the political, economic and social problems of society, Qadhdhafi is convinced that it represents a secular interpretation of basic Islamic principles. The main purposes of Islam are to achieve social justice and to alleviate oppression and tyranny. Another Islamic principle is the unity of faith and social concern. All of these principles are basic to *The Green Book*.

It has been noted that Qadhdhafi rejects what he calls 'positive' or man-made laws, which reflect only the thinking of the individual or group responsible for them, or the interests of a political party, social group or religious sect or school. The primary sources of the law of society for non-Muslims are, as we have seen, social customs (*'urf*) and religion. But when speaking to a Muslim audience, as he did when addressing the foreign ministers of the Muslim world in May 1977, Mu'ammar al-Qadhdhafi could unequivocally declare: 'We bought the Qur'an forth and made it our law, not only because it is the Qur'an, or only because we are Muslims, but also because this source is one which no man can alter or change. The retributive laws, answers to important issues, and directives which it contains are not subject to change by anyone who may gather together a group of people and demand that a single verse be altered.' This fact, Qadhdhafi insisted, will in itself eventually move the Muslim masses everywhere to strive for the creation of a firm and universal law based on the Qur'an. This would in turn ensure progress because 'the Muslim peoples are still living in the ages of feudalism and exploitation'.[51]

For the last two hundred years or more, Muslims have been put on the defensive by the economic, military and colonial ambitions of a reawakened and vibrant Western world. The only historic basis of confidence and renewed hope has been Islam as a faith, civilization and base of power. Yet even Islam, after a spectacular golden age of power and creativity, has succumbed to foreign influences which made it appear to the modern scientific mind as an outdated religion dominated by superstitious myths and legends. Thus Qadhdhafi himself has often admitted in his public speeches that his revolutionary efforts are a reaction to this Western assault on Islam: its scriptures, value system and people. The only way, he asserts, for Muslims to deal with this challenge is to return to their roots, to evolve their own ideological answers to their own problems.

The creation of the Jamahiriyah or 'popular republic' was announced on 2 March 1977, on the Prophet's birthday. On that occasion, after the declaration of the new name of the country, it was stated that the Qur'an is the official law (*shari'a*) of Libya. In a political symposium held in Tripoli on 26 October 1972, Qadhdhafi declared: 'We take the Qur'an as the basic guide for life because it is a perfect Qur'an; because it is a guiding light, and because in it are to be found the solutions to the personal problems of human beings, as well as answers to international issues.' He continued: 'Both the East and West, wishing to obscure our identity, have concentrated their attacks in a dangerous way on the Qur'an. They have concentrated their assaults on our religion by linking it to reactionary and backward superstitions, so that we have ourselves reverted to the idolatrous society which existed before the rise of Islam.'[52]

Qadhdhafi is aware of the importance of international relations, and of the need of the Muslim world for Western technology. He thus observes that, even though Muslims may wish to be independent, they still need to interact with others and benefit from their experiences and let them benefit from their own. He also insists, however, 'That we not allow ourselves to cease to exist, so that in the end someone else may attempt to rebuild us again from zero, and restructure us anew – we refuse this because such a restructuring will in the end make of us slaves in the hands of those who "recreated" us. We are slaves only to God, for He it is who created us.'[53] Muslims must, therefore, reject books and political theories written or arrived at under the influence of the social decadence resulting from the alienation of the machine age. Instead, Muslims must return to the original source of their morality and spiritual well-being. 'We are a nation with a special mission, possessing a Book which was sent down from heaven, a Book in which we all believe.' Muslims must seek in the Qur'an all the laws which they need. Qadhdhafi challenges the students of the social and natural sciences to look for the bases of these disciplines in the Qur'an: 'Anyone who does not know true economics – let him look in the Qur'an where he will find true socialism. Anyone who wishes to study astronomy should know that its basic principles are to be found in the Qur'an. Anyone who seeks the laws that govern human societies in times of war and peace, and which govern international relations – let him look in the Qur'an, for they are there.' 'The Qur'an', Qadhdhafi concludes, 'is a guide to life for the entire world.'[54]

Muslims have generally believed that the Qur'an is in essence eternal. Qadhdhafi reiterates this view by asserting that the Qur'an transcends time and space. The principles and precepts which it contains are eternal verities, 'from which we can obtain our laws and [spiritual] guidance.'[55]

Qadhdhafi can hardly be accused of being a literalist in his approach to Islam and the Qur'an. On the contrary, he counsels Muslims not to take a naïve attitude towards the Qur'an in adopting it as the basis of the law of their society. Rather, the way in which Qur'anic precepts could be implemented should be carefully debated by all members of society. Only then can laws be drafted in broad outline in accordance with the Qur'an by the General People's Congress. The General Secretariat of the Congress would then codify these laws, but without adding anything on their own initiative. Finally, the head of the Congress would affix his signature to these laws, which would henceforth become binding on all the people.[56]

Muslims have traditionally closely identified the Prophet Muhammad with the Qur'an. The Qur'an itself lends support to this identification in many places. It declares the Prophet to be a man of great character.[57] It further asserts: 'Your companion [Muhammad] has surely not gone astray, or erred; nor does he speak out of caprice.'[58] It enjoins the Muslims to 'obey God and obey the Messenger', to accept that which the Messenger gives them, and to desist from anything which he may forbid them.[59]

While he lived, the Prophet was the head of the Muslim community and its guide. He was its military leader and statesman, but above all he was the link between humanity and God. This is most emphatically expressed in the *shahadah* (the formula of witness): 'There is no god but Allah and Muhammad is the messenger of Allah.' His judgement on any matter was final. 'By your Lord', the Qur'an declares, addressing Muhammad, 'they shall not have faith until they accept you as judge over them and find no blame in what you decide.'[60]

The Prophet continues to occupy this high status in the community through his life-example: his words and actions, and even his silent approval of the acts of his companions. This is known as the *sunnah*: way, practice or tradition of the Prophet. Muslims have sharply differed, however, on the veneration of the Prophet and other righteous men and women (*awliya'*) who are regarded as the 'friends', or righteous servants of God. The Qur'an bids the Prophet declare: 'I am a mortal man like you.'[61] Hence the humanity of the Prophet is one of his essential characteristics, and an important element of the faith of Islam.

Libyan society, like that of the rest of North Africa, was dominated before the revolution by Sufi piety. Although Sufism has enriched Islamic spirituality with its deep devotion and artistic creativity, it often degenerated into cults of devotion both to the Prophet and to saints. Like many orthodox Muslim intellectuals, Mu'ammar al-Qadhdhafi has vehemently objected to such Sufi excesses. He fears that Muslims are in danger of deifying Muhammad just as Christians have deified Jesus. In a speech delivered on the occasion of the Prophet's birthday, 12 Rabi' al-Awwal 1398/19 February 1978, he objected: 'The prophet Muhammad never told us that he was the lord of the universe, or that he is the master of all creatures.' He then asked: 'Where did these notions then come from?' Qadhdhafi then challenged his fellow Muslims, saying: 'Search the Qur'an from its beginning to its end! You will find nothing in it of this kind.' The companions, Qadhdhafi argued, used to address the Prophet only with the phrase, 'O messenger of God'. Nor did the early Caliphs use the phrase 'our master' in addressing the Prophet Muhammad. These words are used to address the kings of our time, and God alone is 'the Lord of great sovereignty over the universe'.[62]

The main task of the Prophet, Qadhdhafi further argued, was to convey the message – that is, the Qur'an – which he was commanded by God to follow as much as any other Muslim: 'Follow that which has been revealed to you by your Lord, for God is surely aware of all that you do.'[63] Thus Qadhdhafi has insisted that Muslims should return to the Qur'an alone. They should accept Muhammad merely as a Prophet. What he calls 'the right presentation of Islam' means to reject anything which is not rational, and anything which is metaphysical or hagiographical with regard to the Prophet.[64]

During a frank debate between Colonel Qadhdhafi and a group

of Muslim traditional religious scholars (*ulama'*), held in Tripoli on 3 July 1978, he argued at great length against accepting the *hadith* as a source of guidance beside the Qur'an. His views of the *hadith* are again not new in both the Muslim community and among Western scholars. He was asked by Shaykh Hashim al-A'zami of Iraq: 'What are the sources of legislation which you intend to implement now? Are they both the Book and *sunnah* or the Book alone?' Qadhdhafi answered, 'As for the Book, we are all in agreement concerning it, but with regard to the *sunnah*: can you tell me what the *sunnah* is?' The Shaykh then gave the standard definition of the *sunnah* as the words, actions and consent of the Prophet. Qadhdhafi, however, questioned the authenticity of all the *hadith* traditions attributed to the Prophet. He cast doubt on the authenticity of all that is in the *Sahih* collections of Muslim and Bukhari, these being the two most respected canonical *hadith* collections. These are books, he argued, which have been subject to interpolations and alterations, and thus could not be trusted to preserve the sayings of the Prophet in all their details. He concluded:

Were we to know for certain that this or that *hadith* had been uttered by the Messenger, we would accept it willingly as we would the Qur'an. But the great dilemma is: Where is that which the Messenger actually uttered, and where is that which he did not utter? This is especially serious because after the Messenger, many sects and schools [*madhahib*] appeared in Islam. These schools which you now follow were not present at the time of the Messenger. These schools and sects were political movements which appeared [and later crystallized] in the Muslim community. These sectarian movements brought the Muslims into such great conflicts that the blood of many people was shed, and even the Companions fought among themselves. During this period many *hadiths* were fabricated and falsely attributed to the Messenger in order that every group or party could use these *hadiths* to prove that their stance was the true and Islamic one.

All kinds of people entered into these groups and parties: the hypocritical and wicked as well as the honest and good. Qadhdhafi then concluded: 'If we were now to study the corpus of *hadith* literature, we would find sixty kinds of *hadith*.'[65]

Qadhdhafi gave a few examples of what he considers as contradictory *hadith* to illustrate his point, and argued that the Prophet could not have said one thing and its opposite. One of the participants observed that the *sunnah* is that which agrees in principle with the Qur'an. Qadhdhafi retorted: 'Let us then gather together all the *hadiths* which are said to be [true] and compare them with the Qur'an. Let us then accept all those which agree with the Qur'an and discard those which do not, and no longer speak of Bukhari and Muslim.' Anyone can even now, Qadhdhafi argued further, bring *hadiths* and claim them to be true and sound, but no one can claim a verse to be of the Qur'an if in fact it is not.[66] The Shaykh observed that the method of collecting, codifying and determining the validity of any given *hadith* is an exact science. Those who developed this science, the Shaykh insisted, were sincere in their commitment to serve Islam and not politics. This of course, is true, and the fact that classical *hadith* scholars exercised great caution in admitting the validity of any *hadith* speaks well for their sincerity of faith. It would be a great loss for Muslims to abandon such a rich source of devotional and moral support in the face of adversity and sorrow.

Qadhdhafi admits that *hadith* tradition is an important Islamic and religious heritage. He goes further: 'Everyone of us should be free to implement or reject any *hadith*. Everyone should use his reason in judging among the different *hadiths*. Those which he finds to be good, he must accept, and those which he deems to be weak and false, he should reject. This is the best way because then no one would need to abandon the *hadith* altogether, and no one would impose *hadith* on us.'[67]

Qadhdhafi obviously rejects the *hadith* because of the necessary doubt surrounding the transmission and authenticity of any given *hadith*. He draws an interesting, but somewhat arbitrary, distinction between *hadith* and *sunnah*. It is arbitrary because the Prophet taught both by example and discourse. Moreover, the Muslim community has reached consensus regarding the nature and scope of the *sunnah*, which includes both the Prophet's words and deeds. Qadhdhafi says, '*Sunnah* is not speech.' He explains further: 'When we talk about the *sunnah* of the Prophet, this means his conduct. It means his way; the attitudes which he adopted towards any given matter. The *sunnah* of the Messenger is that he led the Muslims in the morning prayers as two *rak'ahs* [prayer units], four *rak'ahs* for the noon prayers and so on. He also taught them to offer prayers of supererogation [*nawafil*].' Qadhdhafi feels that actions could be transmitted more faithfully, and rightly so, because they are more universally attested. Thus, he argues, Muslims have transmitted the prayers across the centuries as the Prophet performed them, as he was the first *imam*, or prayer leader of the Muslims. Qadhdhafi objects: 'Confusing *sunnah* with *hadith* would be contrary to logic.'[68]

Qadhdhafi again concedes that if he could be totally sure that a *hadith* is the words of the Prophet, he would memorize it and implement it, exactly as he would the Qur'an. It may be important to observe that the first Muslims were reluctant to record and disseminate *hadiths* precisely because they did not want the words of the Prophet to be confused with the words of the Qur'an. Perhaps Qadhdhafi did not mean his words here literally. Without the *hadith*, even the fundamentals of Islam would have remained only Qur'anic moral imperatives without practical application. Qadhdhafi observed, 'We cannot distinguish the sound from the fabricated *hadiths*. The sayings of the Prophet were collected in the second century, hence no one of those who collected *hadith* had been a contemporary of the Prophet.' He thus concluded: '*Hadith* cannot, therefore, serve as "the law of society".'[69]

Qadhdhafi regards everything apart from the Qur'an to be the work of man, and therefore unsuitable as a primary source of the 'natural law of society'. He considers all the legal schools (*madhahib*) of Islam to be 'positive laws'. He says: 'It is this way in which all schools of thought begin: as part of a strictly secular and materialistic law. They are exactly like the Roman law or the Code Napoléon.' This means that every great classical jurist, such as Ibn Hanbal, Malik, and so on, had his own personal considered opinions (*ijtihadat*). These together form what has come to be known as the *shari'ah*, or sacred law of Islam. From this it follows that the *shari'ah* itself, apart from the Qur'an, is a body of 'positive' or man-made laws. In fact Qadhdhafi did announce to the assembled religious scholars: 'I consider the Islamic *shari'ah* as a legal school of thought, exactly like the Roman law or any other law. It is a part of the Islamic heritage; it is not, however, religion.'[70]

Mu'ammar al-Qadhdhafi is not an Islamic jurist, philosopher or theologian. He is a revolutionary thinker and political reformer. Like all revolutionary thinkers, he is impatient with tradition and its inability to keep pace with the demands for change dictated by the space and computer age. His apparently radical ideas regarding the *sunnah* of the Prophet and the *shari'ah* were no doubt inspired by the fact that he was addressing a particular audience. They are far from his answer to Arab students given in the same year, asserting that the Qur'an and *sunnah*, including *hadith*, are primary sources of the 'natural law of Islamic society'. Nor is Qadhdhafi unaware of the fact that the Qur'an in itself is not a law code, but rather a source of law, as has already been observed. It is, in our view, not Qadhdhafi's religious ideas, but his idiom which has made him such a controversial figure.

In his debate with religious leaders, Qadhdhafi defended Mustafa Kamal Ataturk who, in his view, was forced to abandon Islam in favour of Western secularism by the fanatical *ulama'* of his country: 'Fanatics have been disaster for Islam.' Qadhdhafi puts his own words in Ataturk's mouth: 'a religion which will fetter me, and will not allow me to do what is necessary for Turkey to face her enemies and rise up again: I do not want such a religion.'[71] Qadhdhafi considers Ataturk to have been wronged by the fanatical Muslims of his own people. He considers Ataturk's endeavour to save his nation to be a good Islamic action, even though Ataturk reduced the role of Islam. It is clear, however, from Qadhdhafi's Islamic views that he is opposed to Ataturk's departure from basic Islamic practices, and especially his programme of Westernization. In his remarks he only aims to show how the fanaticism of certain *ulama'* could drive any reformer to such extreme measures.

Qadhdhafi's impatience and the criticisms of the fanatics among his own Arab brothers have not, and it is hoped will not, draw him away from Islam. Qadhdhafi is a modernist Muslim who rejects the distinction between the religious and secular in Islam. This is clear from the way in which he has interpreted specific Islamic laws and traditions. Two examples will suffice to illustrate this point.

In November 1971, Qadhdhafi delivered the sermon of '*id al-fitr*, the feast of the end of Ramadan. It was a time of religious as well as national celebration. The Libyan flag had replaced those of Italy, Britain and the United States, as Libya was at long last free from foreign domination. In his sermon, Qadhdhafi announced that the Revolutionary Command Council had issued new legislation regulating the distribution of *zakat* (obligatory alms). This law stipulated that *zakat* in all forms must be organized and placed in a central treasury in order for the government to spend this wealth on care of the poor and on public projects. He declared *zakat* to be the Islamic social security system in its highest meaning, a system of social security and justice which was divinely instituted fourteen hundred years ago.

Qadhdhafi noted that some Arab newspapers have criticized his idea of equating *zakat* with social security, as the latter was a Western system. His remarks in reply to this criticism reflect the spirit of confidence which the revolution has evoked in the Libyan people, especially after the withdrawal of foreign troops from their country. He said: 'Muslim brothers, *zakat* is the implementation of social justice in Islam. This justice which the modern world considers as one of the fundamental bases of socialism, we discovered first centuries ago.' In support of this claim he quoted the Qur'anic verse: 'And those of whose wealth there is a specified portion – for the beggar and the needy'.[72] He then asked: 'Who is the beggar, and who is the needy?' 'They are', he answered, 'the toiling workers, the poor who are now called the oppressed classes. It is these oppressed classes whom we regard as the beggars and the needy.' Colonel Qadhdhafi then expressed his enthusiasm for the revolution, for Islam and for the Arab nation as follows:

> We are a great nation with an eternal mission, a nation
> which taught humanity that which it did not know. This
> verse means that the state, with the authority of the law, can
> take from the exploiting capitalists and give to the poor and
> needy. This verse gives the ruler the legitimate permission
> to issue whatever laws he sees necessary for the curtailment
> or control of the people's wealth and exploitation. This is
> because the poor and needy have a right to this wealth. All
> wealth belongs to God, and human beings are his
> representatives on earth.'[73]

In the Qur'anic principle of *zakat* and other forms of almsgiving, Qadhdhafi bases his theory of 'Islamic socialism', which will be considered later in this discussion.

One of the most controversial Islamic practices has been polygamy. It may be argued that polygamy is recommended in the Qur'an not as a law or duty, but as a necessary solution to an important social problem: the problem of female orphans. When a law was formed, however, to answer this legitimate concern, humanitarian dimensions were lost sight of completely. Polygamy thus became a social custom or tradition in Muslim society, and it is as such that Colonel Qadhdhafi treats it.

He begins his discussion with the assertion that polygamy is not enjoined in the Qur'an, but allowed only conditionally. 'The Qur'an states: "If you fear that you cannot deal justly with female orphans, then marry what pleases you: two, three or four; but if you fear that you cannot treat them equally, then only one". The Qur'an, moreover, adds in a later verse of the same *surah* that if a man fears he may wrong female orphans, the solution is to marry them: be they two, three or four. But if the marriage which is intended to solve this problem does not in fact solve it, and the wrong continues, then there is no reason for marrying more than one woman from among them. This is the only situation where God allows a man to marry two, three or four women. Otherwise, there is no verse which permits polygamy.'[75]

Qadhdhafi argues further that if man is allowed more than one wife, then the woman must also have the right to more than one husband. Of course, he insists, civilized societies would not tolerate this practice. Polygamy is therefore only the exception, but monogamy is the norm.[76] The practice of multiple marriages in Muslim society has been a problem for many modernist thinkers. Muhammad 'Abduh, the great Egyptian reformer, said concerning this thorny problem: 'No one can discipline a society in this day and age in which polygamy is widespread.'[77]

Two important questions remain for us to consider. The first is: why does Qadhdhafi insist on the Qur'an as the fundamental constitution of his revolutionary society? This question is important because he could have claimed, as have other Muslim revolutionary thinkers, to be within the framework of Islam without specifically insisting on the primacy of the Qur'an in his ideology. The second, closely related question is: What is the relationship of *The Green Book* to the Qur'an? In other words, if *The Green Book* is based on the Qur'an, then why does it make no reference to it; and if it is not, then is it actually meant to supplant the Qur'an? Colonel Qadhdhafi himself raises these questions and answers them.

Qadhdhafi gives several reasons for his choice of the Qur'an as 'the law of society'. The first is that, because the Qur'an is the Word of God, it is eternal. Its precepts, injunctions and laws relate not only to the life to come, but to this life as well. Thus marriage and divorce, alimony and inheritance, theft and adultery are all regulated in the Qur'an. There is, therefore, no need to seek other laws and personal opinions to deal with these issues. The second reason given by Qadhdhafi is that the laws of the Qur'an regarding the life to come with its rewards and punishments are necessary for the building of a good and virtuous society, a society that seeks the good and avoids evil. Thirdly, he argues that the Qur'an also contains the general principles of social harmony, morality and goodness. It teaches us not to transgress against others or to show malice, not in the hereafter, but in this life.

These Qur'anic principles, Qadhdhafi observes, are universal limits (*hudud*) governing human conduct. The law which they engender is a law of non-aggression. The Qur'an says: 'O you who have faith, let not any people mock other people, for perhaps they may be better than them. Nor let any woman mock other women, for perhaps they may be better than them. Do not slander one another, nor should you despise one another through name-calling.'[78] Qadhdhafi offers the following interesting interpretation of this verse: 'This means let no social class enslave another.' Through this injunction, he concludes, 'the Qur'an permits revolution against slavery'.[79]

Fourthly, the Qur'an has decreed that four months of every lunar year shall be sacred months.[80] During these months war, as well as any other form of aggression, is prohibited. Were all nations to follow this decree, then the entire world would benefit from the spirit of the Qur'an. This spirit Qadhdhafi characterizes thus: 'He who believes in the Qur'an would conduct himself well. He would not transgress against others; he would not oppress others; nor would he devour the wealth of others wrongfully.'[81]

The fifth Qur'anic principle in which Qadhdhafi finds support for his socialist ideal is that of spending of one's wealth in the way of God. 'The Qur'an', he argues, 'strictly forbids hoarding of any kind. This is expressed in the stern warning: "Those who hoard gold and silver, and do not spend of it for the cause of God – announce to them a painful torment." '[82] Gold and silver, Qadhdhafi argues, include today's hard currencies which are smuggled out of the country in dollars and deposited in foreign banks. Rather, he insists: 'Work and eat! Work and consume! Then anything you have beyond your immediate needs, does not belong to you.'[83] One of the religious scholars present interrupted here with the Qur'anic verse 'God has preferred some of you over others with His bounty.'[84] But Qadhdhafi replied: 'There are verses in the Qur'an which describe an existing situation, but this does not mean that it is the right situation. This only means that there was a given situation at the time when the Qur'an was sent down.'[85]

There is no doubt that the main purpose of the Qur'an, and indeed of the entire mission of the Prophet Muhammad, was to reform society on all levels, and to guide it to God and to the good. The Qur'an, however, recognizes differences among the poor and the rich in society. It seeks not to abolish these differences, but to place them within the moral and spiritual perspective of the Islamic faith and order. The Qur'anic statement under discussion is not descriptive but prescriptive, as the verse goes on to direct how this wealth should be spent.

Mu'ammar al-Qadhdhafi is right in observing that Muslims have often used this and other verses like it in the Qur'an to argue for flagrant injustice and exploitation of the poor and downtrodden of society. He asks: 'Is religion then slaves and servants, maidservants and numerous wives? Is it big palaces and tall buildings? Is it spending the fast of Ramadan in Germany and making the *hajj* pilgrimage by way of Rome?' 'Is it', he concludes, 'big bellies and bulging pockets? Is this religion? No, I seek refuge in God! If this is what religion is, by God, I will abandon it before morning. On the contrary, I am sure that the exact opposite is true! Religion came to abolish all such rotten things.'[86] The Arabian peninsula, Qadhdhafi adds, was dominated by such evil practices. Thus when Muhammad came only the weak and oppressed of society accepted him. With them he fought oppression and wrongdoing until Bilal, the black slave, was equal with Umayyah, the rich man of Quraysh who was his master. Islam, Qadhdhafi concludes, is the religion of equality and liberty; it is against bourgeois society.

If the Qur'an has all that humanity needs for the attainment of a good, just and spiritually sound society, then why *The Green Book*? In August 1982, Qadhdhafi addressed the second conference of the Islamic Call Society, discussing *The Green Book*, its purpose and its relation to the Qur'an and the Prophetic *hadith* Tradition. He first argued that it is imperative, if Muslims are to achieve a just society with equality among all its members, then they must all participate in attaining this goal. This participation is possible only if the principle of consultation (*shura*) is followed. This principle is stated in the Qur'anic phrase 'and their affairs are decided through consultation amongst themselves'.[87] Qadhdhafi argues: 'Consultation means all the Muslims, not simply a group of them. There is no other way but that all Muslims must engage in consultation. The only way they can all engage in consultation is through people's congresses. For this reason the first part of *The Green Book* discusses the organization and operation of people's congresses.'[88]

The second part of *The Green Book*, Qadhdhafi explained, is meant to effect equality and social justice among all peoples of the world. The third part in particular is meant to rectify deviations in society from the Qur'an. But, he argues,

> It was not necessary that we write in it [*The Green Book*], 'the Prophet said "all men are equal, like the teeth of a comb".' Nor was it necessary for us to write, "Anyone who goes to sleep sated while his neighbor is hungry, is not one of us". Had we done this, *The Green Book* would have been simply a *hadith* book, or at least a book which only Muslims would read. Non-Muslims would see these references to the *hadith* and say, 'This is a book for Muslims only'.

Qadhdhafi goes on to state that his *Green Book* is intended primarily as a scientific attempt at finding solutions to the political, economic and social problems of the modern world. As such, it could be accepted by anyone. 'When, however, a reader of *The Green Book* recognizes that it is a book of great benefit, we can then tell him, "This is a part of the great bounty of Islam, which is God's favor towards you." This is our answer to those who ask why Qadhdhafi does not quote verses from the Qur'an in his *Green Book*.'[89]

In itself *The Green Book* cannot serve as a law or constitution encompassing all the problems and affairs of society. Hence, it was felt necessary that an institute dedicated to the study and research of all aspects of *The Green Book* be established. It is hoped that this Institute will devote time and effort to the Islamic applications, problems and adjustments contained in *The Green Book* which are relevant to Muslim societies today.

Thus the Third Universal Theory which *The Green Book* propounds is presented not as a new doctrine to supersede or supplant Islam, but as a new and contemporary interpretation of the Qur'an's social message. Mu'ammar al-Qadhdhafi asserted in September 1972, when the Third Universal Theory was still in the making, that it was not a new message, 'because there is no message after the message of the apostle Muhammad'.[90] The Third Universal Theory is a political theory with important Islamic dimensions. It is to these dimensions that we must now turn.

Islam and the Political Challenge

No religious tradition, and Islam in particular, can be reduced to a
mere set of beliefs and practices. The impassioned objections which
Qadhdhafi raised to the assembled *ulama'* concerning the prevalent
view of Islam today could be summed up in a view of Islam as an
important catalyst of reform and social change, rather than as a
system able to serve the limited interests of one decadent class in
society. It is on this practical social level that the roles of religion
and politics become closely interrelated. The issue of the role of
religion in society is especially important for the Muslim community, which refuses to separate its faith from its social and
political affairs, in spite of the criticisms of traditional Islam both by
Western and Muslim intellectuals and political thinkers.
Qadhdhafi's view of Islam and its function as an instrument of
progress and revolutionary change is typical of all movements of
Islamic revival.

Qadhdhafi believes that Islam, which provided the basis and
impetus for a rich, prosperous and strong Muslim community in the
past, is still capable of raising Muslim society now to its former state
of power and glory. This he succinctly expressed in his address in
July 1983, to a youth gathering in Moravia. He began by insisting
that Islam must be politically effective. A person's faith and observance of the fundamentals of Islam will be well rewarded by God,
but this in itself is not sufficient. It is necessary for Islam to be an
effective basis of collective action among Muslim nations,
Qadhdhafi argued. These nations must support all revolutionary
liberation movements, regardless of whether they are or are not
Islamic. He voiced disappointment with the fact that non-Muslim
countries in Africa are progressive, while Muslim countries are
generally reactionary, serving the interests of imperialism and
colonialism. 'Islam must', Colonel Qadhdhafi asserted, 'constitute
a united political power capable of safeguarding the interests of its
adherents, so long as they are Muslims united by a common faith, a
common scripture, a common Prophet and a common *qiblah*
[direction of prayer]. These common religious factors must in the
end be translated into political activity that would defend the people
of this faith, protect them and create in them a sense of fraternal
responsibility towards one another. Otherwise, Islam would mean
nothing to its people.'[91]

Islamic traditions, practices and important occasions must, Qadhdhafi believes, be used to strengthen the political and social bond among Muslims. In a sermon which he delivered on the occasion of *'id al-adha* (feast of sacrifice) in November 1978, he argued, 'As for the prayers of the two *'ids*, they are a conference which brings Muslims together.' (They are usually performed in the open, so as to allow the largest possible number of people to participate in them.) In the mosque, he further argued, the world must be left behind, and only the name of God is to be remembered. But in this open 'conference of worship', Qadhdhafi asserted, 'We must also discuss politics, social issues, and all our wordly affairs and problems.' 'Why is it', he then asked, 'that the *ummah* of Muhammad is backward today?'[92]

This question has occupied Muslim thinkers and political activists for centuries. It may be argued that all Islamic political and religious revivalist movements in the last century and a half have been attempts at providing answers to this problem. Qadhdhafi asks himself also why the nations surrounding the Muslim world possess the technological and economic power to threaten the very existence of the Muslim community. Some have thought that Islam is itself a backward and primitive religion, and thus have abandoned it. Yet, Qadhdhafi observed, the nations which have abandoned Islam have not progressed; they remain as they were before. The problem, therefore, is not the Islamic faith. The Qur'an declares, 'We have sent down the Book to you [Muhammad], an elucidation of everything: a guidance and mercy, and glad tidings to Muslims.'[93] Qadhdhafi comments: 'This verse assures us that the Book which was sent down to the Muhammadan *ummah* contains scientific knowledge, guidance and glad tidings of goodness and happiness. Hence, the backwardness of the Muslims in the modern age has nothing to do with Islam.'[94]

Qadhdhafi sees three main causes contributing to the decline of Islamic civilization and power in modern times. First, 'Crusader colonialism, both old and new' has played an important part in this decline. It is, therefore, a binding duty on all Muslims, from Indonesia to Morocco, to carry out 'a holy struggle' in the cause of revolution and liberation.

The second factor is what Qadhdhafi calls 'making Islam, the word of truth, serve a false purpose'. This refers to the static and traditional mentality which fails to set Islam against the amassing of great and illegitimate wealth, or the acquisition of large palaces with numerous servants. Citing a powerful Qur'anic reproach against glorying in vain wealth and healthy children,[95] Qadhdhafi insists that Islam is not simply wealth, sons and wives. Rather, 'Islam is a revolution calling people to progress, to freedom and to constructive work. Islam requires that you work for your faith as though you were going to die tomorrow, and that you work for the good of your life here on earth as though you were going to live forever.'[96] Qadhdhafi thus equates immorality or lewd behaviour (*fisq*), which Islam strongly condemns, with capitalism. In support of this assertion, he again cites the Qur'an: 'When We wish to destroy a town, We give free rein to the rich among its inhabitants, and they lead dissolute lives in it! Thus just judgment would be passed over them, and We destroy it utterly.'[97]

Colonel Qadhdhafi is convinced that the sad state of Muslim society today is the result of political conditions which colonialism created in the Muslim world. Thus true Islam must be a world-wide armed revolution against enslavement and oppression. The Qur'an urges the people of faith to engage in this fight: 'Prepare all the power you can against them.'[98] Qadhdhafi interprets this Qur'anic injunction as a call to arms, a call to general conscription, a call to general military training. 'It is a call to this community to be strong.'[99]

Islam is not against scientific progress, such as the exploration of space, landing on the moon, or making artificial rain. This is because God is the creator of all these things, and He has subjected all things to man. Still some hypocritical Muslims, Qadhdhafi angrily objects, say, 'These are forbidden by God [*haram*].' He went on: 'We here in Libya are not ashamed of championing a progressive and highly leftist revolution! But we shall never compromise Islam, in order to supposedly demonstrate to the world that the backwardness which has afflicted Muslims has no relation to Islam. On the contrary, Islam leads people to progress.' Islam itself was a revolution, and the Prophet, Qadhdhafi argued, was himself a revolutionary leader. He revolted against Umayyah, Abu Jahl, Abu Lahab and Abu Sufyan. These were the men of power and wealth among the Arabs. They stand for the kings, princes and emperors of all human societies, Qadhdhafi concluded.[100]

The third cause of the backwardness of Muslims, Qadhdhafi asserts, is that 'they have forgotten a portion of that which they received of the Remembrance'. Qadhdhafi here borrows a Qur'anic reproach directed at the People of the Book for neglecting a portion of their own scriptures.[101] God, Qadhdhafi argues, chose the Muslim community to be the bearer of His last message to humankind. This great challenge is stated in the Qur'anic verse: 'You are the best community brought forth for humankind – you enjoin the good, dissuade from evil and have faith in God.'[102] Because Muslims have neglected the demands of their faith, God has become wrathful with them. The consequences of his Divine wrath have been backwardness: hunger, disease, reactionism and dictatorship. This has also resulted in their subjugation to foreign powers.[103]

Qadhdhafi, however, sees in the revolution of his own country a new hope. He constantly reminds his fellow Muslims of the golden age of Islamic civilization when Muslims led the world in all the sciences, philosophy and religious knowledge. Muslims must regain their place of prominence in technology and learning.

An important aspect of any revolution is the call for radical change and breaking with tradition. In advocating change, Qadhdhafi has been guided by the aims and objectives of the revolution of 1 September. If the prayers of the two great Muslim festivals of *al-fitr* and *al-adha* could be regarded as Muslim conferences, the *hajj* pilgrimage to Makkah and Madinah is a unique international conference to which Muslims come from the four corners of the earth. They come to renew their allegiance to God, to their faith and history. The *hajj* has been a veritable Islamic forum where many historic decisions and religious and political movements were born. Recognizing this fact, Qadhdhafi has called for the freedom of the holy cities of Makkah and Madinah from the control of any one state or political power. He has suggested the creation of an international committee representing most, if not all, of the Muslim states, to manage the pilgrimage and administer the two holy cities. This would give all Muslims the right to make the pilgrimage, even those who may be at war or in conflict with any of the nations represented on that committee. He further suggested that any Muslim wishing to make the pilgrimage be allowed to travel to the holy cities without a visa.[104]

A significant example of Qadhdhafi's break with tradition and the consensus of Muslims for almost all of their history is his change of the Muslim calendar. He recommends that Muslims use not the *hijrah*, or migration of the Prophet from Makkah to Madinah, as the start of their history, but rather the date of the death of the Prophet. Qadhdhafi made the same recommendation to the second conference of the Arab ministers of culture, held in Tripoli in February 1979. Libya has since adopted the new method of dating.

The *hijrah* of the Prophet, Qadhdhafi notes, did not take place on the 1 Muharram, the first month of the Muslim calendar, but perhaps on the 12 Rabi' al-Awwal, nearly two and a half months later. Thus the present Islamic dating is, in any case, inaccurate. More important than the *hijrah*, however, Qadhdhafi contends, is the death of the Prophet. He said: 'Thus because our Apostle was the seal of the prophets, his death meant the cessation of revelation, or the end of direct communication between heaven and earth. Heaven no longer communicated with the earth because there was no prophet after him.' Muhammad's death is, therefore, for Qadhdhafi, a very important event which should have been precisely dated and used as the focus of Muslim history. It would have been better to link the year of the Muslim calendar to this most important event of Muslim history, particularly since it is believed that the Prophet died in the same month in which he migrated. If the two events happened at approximately the same time of the month, then the more important of the two must be chosen. The death of the Prophet is of far greater significance than his migration, Qadhdhafi believes.[105]

Qadhdhafi has further argued that the conquest of Makkah is also of greater significance than the *hijrah*. This is because this meant the purification of the House of God (the Kab'ah) from the filth of idols. Here again, Qadhdhafi's primary motivation in changing the present Islamic dating appears to be a new and all-inclusive Islamic revolution. He thus asserted, 'now that we are in the process of rectifying Islamic history and reviving a new civilization, I would not hesitate in saying that *hijrah* dating was not correct. The right way would have been for us either to date from the death of the Messenger, or the conquest of Makkah, or that the first of Muharram be kept as the beginning of the new lunar year only.'[106] Another argument against *hijrah* dating is that it is a 'positive' or man-made law which the second Caliph 'Umar ibn al-Khattab arbitrarily imposed on the Muslim community.[107] Qadhdhafi also fears that with the passing of time and the rise of various personality cults in Islam, there is a real danger of forgetting the significance of the event of revelation, and hence a danger of an overshadowing of the Qur'an's role as the law of society by the lives of such saints and messianic figures. It is because of this that he insists on stressing the importance of the death of the Prophet and hence of the cessation of revelation for Muslim history.

It is important to observe that the migration of the Prophet and his small following from Makkah to Madinah marked the beginning of an Islamic era: the birth of a state, or socio-economic and religio-political entity. It was no doubt for this reason that this event was recognized by the first Muslims as a turning point in their lives and the life of the community. To be sure, the death of the Prophet is of crucial importance. Yet the Prophet died only when his mission was completed, and the Qur'an was also closed.

The *hijrah* as a historic event remains of special significance for Muslim faith and history. But apart from any historical or philosophical considerations, changing the Muslim calendar in this way would create new and complex problems for research in any field of Muslim thought and civilization. This is because the whole heritage of Islam has been dated by the *hijrah*. Thus for anyone to change this time-honoured tradition now after fourteen hundred years, would create many unnecessary difficulties.

Islam and the New Socialism

Three important problems have occupied Muslims throughout their history, and especially in the post-enlightenment age. The first is how to make the Islamic system of faith and practice of the first three centuries of the *hijrah* relevant to the needs of a technologized society a thousand years later. The second is: if Muslims were then to borrow the ideals and ideologies of the developed West, what can they import into the Islamic system without deforming it, or distorting its basic ideals? The third problem, which is closely related, concerns how and to what extent Muslims can and should preserve their classical heritage intact.

Qadhdhafi, as we have clearly seen, is open to radical change and innovation, so long as the Qur'an remains the fundamental guide and constitution of society. Yet the Qur'an, like any sacred scriptures, is open to many and often very different interpretations. In fact Qadhdhafi has repeatedly called for new interpretations of the Qur'an in order that it may provide the basis for radical revolutionary change. It is with this in mind that Qadhdhafi has insisted that the fundamental principles of true socialism are found in the Qur'an. Qadhdhafi's 'new Islamic socialism', while remaining the same in broad outline, has none the less undergone through the years a process of development in orientation and emphasis. In part this development reflects the political and economic relations of Libya with the industrialized world: the United States and Western Europe, and the Soviet Union and Eastern Europe. In a student conference held at the Libyan University in Benghazi on 6 November 1969, Qadhdhafi was asked to define socialism and the means of implementing it. In spite of general opposition to the question by students in the gathering who apparently felt that the answer was all too obvious, the 'leader of the revolution' made the following remarks:

> Our socialism is both Arab and Islamic. We stand midway between socialism and communism and socialism and capitalism. Our socialism springs directly from the needs and requirements of the Arab world, its heritage, and the needs of its society. It consists of a social justice which means sufficiency in production and just distribution. These principles are to be found in the Islamic religion, and particularly in the law of *zakat* [alms]. [108]

The idea of Islamic socialism is not new. Nor was the idea of Arab socialism first propounded by Mu'ammar al-Qadhdhafi. It was his mentor, the champion of Arab socialism, Gamel Nasser, who first made it the ideological basis of his Arab nationalism. Qadhdhafi, however, was the first to speak of the 'Arabo-Islamic socialism' which he made the fundamental ideology of the revolution of 1 September. Socialism is for him the basis of social and political freedom. Socialism in its Arab and Islamic conception 'respects private ownership and regards it as sacred'. [109] Thus what gives this distinctive socialism its Islamic character is its respect for the right of private ownership. It differs completely from the capitalist system in which one class of society dominates all other classes, which it then seeks to crush and humiliate. It is also completely different from the communist system in which a capitalist government dominates all other classes in the name of the workers, and thus establishes a society of state capitalism. True socialism, in contrast, promotes equal opportunity, social justice and the sacred alliance of all the active elements of society. This new socialism represents a 'third power' in the world, a power which refuses to be dominated by either of the two other powers. Qadhdhafi thus concludes: 'Our socialism is the socialism of the Arab nation, the socialism of Islam and the socialism of all the peoples of the Third World.' This is because Islam is the religion of justice, 'the religion of true socialism', according to Qadhdhafi. 'The Qur'an', Qadhdhafi argues, 'advocated socialism long before Marx and Lenin.'[110]

The socialist systems which now exist in the Third World, Qadhdhafi believes, have no real basis in either the culture or religion of the peoples which have adopted them. In the end, therefore, they will either be absorbed by the communist or capitalist systems. It is necessary, therefore, to find a solution which would not ultimately lead to communism or capitalism, but which would instead provide a new basis for a just society. This new basis is the Third Universal Theory.[111]

In an interview with the B.B.C. in April 1976, Qadhdhafi was asked why he would reject communism as a solution to the problems of modern society. He replied: 'Of course, if communism means exclusive state ownership, then we reject such exclusive types of policies. If, moreover, communism means atheism, then we reject this atheism, because we believe in God.' Qadhdhafi then went on to state his rejection of capitalism in the same terms.[112]

It has been realized by many Third World thinkers that colonialism is not simply occupation of the land of others and alien rule and exploitation of the natural and human resources of underdeveloped nations. An equally dangerous form of colonialism consists of the cultural and intellectual domination by one nation of another. Thus Qadhdhafi regards both communism and capitalism as forms of neocolonialism. Russian socialism is at present, in Qadhdhafi's view, also a form of colonialism. This is because anyone who enters the Soviet camp will have to receive orders from Moscow. It is imperative, therefore, he argues, that the Arab and Muslim peoples evolve their own ideology, and not be deceived by anti-imperialist Soviet slogans. It is also important, Qadhdhafi believes, that the mistaken notion that communism and socialism are one and the same thing be exposed.[113]

There is only one true socialism, Qadhdhafi believes. It is neither the socialism of the East nor the socialism of the West, but rather the socialism which is based on Islam. Yet even though Islam remains for Qadhdhafi the main source and inspiration of his socialist ideal, he sees socialism as a truth independent of Islam and existing before it, although one which the Qur'an recognized and confirms.

In an interesting interview with a local Libyan magazine, *al-Majalis al-Musawwarah*, in April 1973, Qadhdhafi made the following statement: 'We need not call socialism "Islamic socialism", or even "Arab socialism". Rather we should call it simply socialism. It is neither communism nor capitalism.' Socialism is for Qadhdhafi an absolute value, just as goodness is an absolute value. He continued: 'Still socialism is inspired by the teachings of Islam, and is found in essence in the Qur'an. This is not to say that socialism came into being after Islam, but rather that it is basically a just system which the Qur'an describes and urges people to follow.' As an absolute value, socialism was before the Qur'an, just as truth was before the Qur'an. Qadhdhafi then gave a specific example to illustrate his point: 'The Qur'an does not lay down a law for things; rather it provides the bases for such laws. By setting forth basic principles, the Qur'an allows people to promulgate laws based on them.'[114]

It has been stressed in this study that Colonel Qadhdhafi is not a philosopher but a revolutionary activist. His ultimate aim in propounding his socialist system was not to present a philosophy, but to implement his ideas and ideals of a just society. In April 1983, in the first international symposium on *The Green Book*, Qadhdhafi offered a concise definition of his theory of the 'new socialism': 'It is in sum that all the wealth of society is to be divided among all its members. This is because, since it is their [the people's] rightful possession, they all have equal rights to it.' In that sense the 'new socialism' is unique, different from both Western and Eastern socialism, as well as the forms of socialism practised in Third World countries. 'Among the basic aims of socialism', Qadhdhafi states, 'is that of turning wage earners into partners.'[115]

Any philosophy or social theory, however universal it may claim to be, must none the less have a cultural soil in which it can grow and be nurtured. Furthermore, most philosophies, however humanistic they may be, nevertheless reflect a national identity, a specific culture and a nationalistic or religious reaction to rival human ideals. Qadhdhafi's aims, ideals and national and religious views are all expressed in the following argument for the 'new Islamic socialism' by a fellow Arab thinker, Salah al-Jibali:

> Islamic laws and principles are the best foundations upon
> which socialism can be established in our lands. These laws
> and principles are also best capable of affirming our

independent national personality, freeing our nation from
intellectual and political subordination to the superpowers
and protecting our masses from Western nations which seek
to conquer the minds of our youth. These principles
represent the strongest response to all the continuous
attempts which aim at dragging us into this or that sphere of
influence, and which seek to distort our Arabic and Islamic
heritage.[116]

The term *ishtirakiyah* (usually translated 'socialism') means literally partaking or sharing. Qadhdhafi has repeatedly insisted that it is
not socialism as understood and practised either in the West or in
the East. Even though this term occurs neither in the Qur'an nor in
the *hadith*, the Islamic principles on which it is based, Qadhdhafi
believes, were closely adhered to in the society of the Prophet and
his immediate successors. Among these principles were private
ownership, collective work or production, and equality and social
justice. The Qur'an does in fact present these principles as moral
imperatives, and the Prophet in his *sunnah* (custom and life
example) did apply them as practical measures in his society.

Private ownership in Islam is regarded essentially as human
stewardship over God's wealth. The Qur'an enjoins: 'Give in alms
of that which God has charged you with as His representatives.'[117]
This means that private ownership is regulated by the general
interests of society, which is in turn expressed through the per-
formance of 'good works' such as the *zakat* and the free-will offering
(*sadaqah*), giving 'in the way of God'. Natural resources are, however, not included in the category of private property because they
belong to society. These would, therefore, be distributed in the
society as its needs and circumstances dictated. An example of this
in the Prophet's community was when the Ansar ('helpers' – that is,
the residents of Madinah who joined with the Prophet after his
migration there) shared their wealth and lands with the Muhajirun
('immigrants' – that is, those who migrated with the Prophet to
Madinah). It is related on the authority of Zayd ibn Aslam, a
well-known companion of the Prophet, that the Prophet said to the
Ansar: 'Your brethren have left their wealth and children and come
to you.' They answered, 'Our lands shall be divided among us to be
cultivated.' But the Prophet insisted: 'These are people who have
no knowledge of working the land. You must therefore release
them from this obligation and still share your crops with them.'[118]

The principle of work or production is governed in Islam by the prohibition of hoarding and usury. It is again a moral imperative demanding the acquisition of only 'lawful profits'. Islam does not allow crop-sharing or feudalism. The Prophet is said to have stipulated: 'Whoever owns land, let him cultivate it! If he cannot, or is physically unable to do so, then let him grant it to his Muslim brother. But let him not lease it out to him.'[119] Thus any profit in Islam must be gained by one's own efforts, not through the efforts of others or the yield of property already owned on which the labour of others is expended. In fact, the principle of work and its recompense in human society is governed by the same Qur'anic principles describing human deeds and their Divine rewards both in this world and the next: 'To each shall be a station in reward for that which he has done. He shall recompense them fully for their works, and they shall not be wronged.'[120] An oft-quoted *hadith* of the Prophet stipulates: 'Give the worker his due before his sweat dries up.'[121]

The principles of human equality and social justice both stem from the moral demands set forth in both the Qur'an and *sunnah*. The Qur'an teaches that all human beings are the progeny of one male and one female, and that they were made into different nations and tribes 'in order that they might know one another'. It then adds: 'Surely the most noble of you in the sight of God is he who is most righteous.[122] Commenting on this verse, the Prophet said, 'God has abolished through Islam the haughtiness of the age of the ignorance [*jahiliyah* – that is, the time in Arabia before the coming of Islam] and their [Arab] boasting of their lineage. This is because all humankind are from Adam, and Adam is of clay. The noblest of them in the sight of God is he who is most righteous.'[123]

True social justice can never be achieved through the blind force of law. It must begin in the consciences of men and women and in their concern for the welfare of others. Those who are truly just are they, the Qur'an says, 'who give of their wealth, though they cherish it, to the orphans, the needy and the wayfarer, and for the ransoming of captives'. Spending one's wealth with sincere concern for the welfare of others is, according to the Qur'an, 'giving God a goodly loan which He will repay in manifold measure'.[124] In more practical terms, the Prophet expressed this concern in the injunction: 'He who has an extra beast of burden, let him give it to one who has no beast of burden. He who has more food than he needs, let him give it to one who has no food.'[125]

The derivation of socialism, or any ideology, from Islam no doubt gives it an authenticity and relevance for millions of pious Muslim men and women. Yet this in itself is not enough. What in the end determines the Islamic character of an ideology is the extent to which it reflects the Islamic spirit of moral uprightness and tolerance. Islam is the religion of equilibrium, of balance between excess and insufficiency in all things. This is the greatest challenge to Muslims today, one posed by the Qur'an itself: 'Thus have we made you a community of the just middle course in order that you may be witnesses over humankind.'[126]

Qadhdhafi, we argued earlier, is a humanist and a man of deep faith. His impatience and at times uncompromising directness may obscure this fact. We have attempted in this chapter to let him speak for the most part of his own faith, hopes and frustrations. We shall end with a telegram which he sent to all the rulers of the world on the occasion of the New Year in 1975:

The people of the earth, and even the angels of heaven have despaired of the meaningless exchange over hundreds of years of the greeting, 'Happy New Year!' Every ruler repeats this greeting, and yet goes on striving to make the year one of misfortune, rather than happiness. Can we, therefore, stop for a moment to ponder some verses of the scriptures: The Qur'an, the Torah, and the Gospels? The Qur'an says, 'Assist one another in works of righteousness and piety, and assist not one another in works of wrongdoing and transgression.'[127] Let us remember how Christ reproached people because they forgot the word of God, and instead gave themselves to conceit. He upbraided the priests for their neglect of God's word and for their greed. He reproached the scribes for spreading false teachings, and for abandoning the law of God. All this he declared in his first sermon which he preached in Jerusalem. Now because we are without a Christ to reproach the conceited, the greedy, those who propagate false teachings and those who oppose God's law, we must reproach one another for our sins. . . . We must realize that we are far removed from the teachings of Christ, and are instead close to the teachings of Satan. The superpowers spend large sums on producing more nuclear bombs and the development of intercontinental missiles. They are engaged in the conquest of space and the spread of propaganda and psychological warfare, while the rest of the people of the globe suffer the scourges of disease, hunger, and rocketing inflation. In reality, these nations are guided by Satan and his scriptures and by the theories of Marx, and not by any holy scripture. We are in great need of the teachings of Christ which would command us saying, 'Lift your hands from Palestine, the birthplace of Christ, peace be upon him, from Ireland, Southeast Asia and your colonies in Africa!' How greatly in need is the world today of Christ, in order that it may turn away from bars and from vain pleasures on every Christmas and New Year. People should instead turn to houses of worship to offer prayers, seek God's forgiveness and reflect upon His law.[128]

With season's greetings.

Notes

1 1 Cor. 13:12 and Qur'an 75:22.
2 *al-Sijill al-Qawmi*, vol. 8 (1976–77), pp. 98–9.
3 These were two powerful but corrupt Arab tribes mentioned in the Qur'an to which God sent messengers; but they rejected them, and were thus destroyed.
4 See, for example, Qur'an 7:65ff. and 41:13ff.
5 Qur'an 9:40.
6 *al-Sijill al-Qawmi*, vol. 2, (1970–71), p. 96.
7 See, for example, Qur'an 10:5, 17:12 and 36:40.
8 *al-Sijill al-Qawmi*, vol. 2, p. 97.
9 See Qur'an 80:1–10; and *al-Sijill al-Qawmi*, vol. 2, pp. 96–103.
10 Qur'an 6:38.
11 *al-Sijill al-Qawmi*, vol. 2, p. 245. See also pp. 233–45.
12 *Ibid.*, vol. 3 (1971–72), p. 224.
13 *Ibid.*, p. 266.
14 *Ibid.*, p. 348.
15 *Ibid.*, p. 361–2.
16 *Ibid.*, vol. 4 (1972–73), p. 18.
17 *Ibid.*, pp. 201–2.
18 Qur'an 99:7 and 9; *al-Sijill al-Qawmi*, vol. 4, p. 24.
19 See *al-Kitab al-Akhdar*, part 3, pp. 123–4, and Chapter 2 above, Solving the Problem of Society.
20 *al-Sijill al-Qawmi*, vol. 4, p. 306.

21 *Khutab wa-Ahadith al-Qa'id al-Diniyah* (Tripoli, al-Quwwat al-Musallahah al-Libiyah, Idarat al-Tawjih al-Ma'nawi, n.d.), p. 117.

22 *Ibid.*, p. 117.

23 *Ibid.*, p. 122.

24 *Ibid.*, p. 141; see also *al-Sijill al-Qawmi*, vol. 8, pp. 682–702.

25 Qur'an 22:78.

26 *al-Sijill al-Qawmi*, vol. 4, pp. 310–12.

27 Qur'an 4:135; *al-Sijill al-Qawmi*, vol. 4, p. 317.

28 *al-Sijill al-Qawmi*, vol. 4, pp. 831–2.

29 See for example, Qur'an 2:13 and 3:51.

30 Qur'an 2:134.

31 Qur'an 29:46.

32 *al-Sijill al-Qawmi*, vol. 4, p. 312.

33 *Ibid.*, p. 316.

34 Qur'an 5:49; see also 5:43, where the Jews of Madinah are upbraided for not judging by the Torah.

35 Much has been written on this thorny issue. See, for a useful summary of Muslim views on the subject, I. Di Matteo, 'Tahrif' od alterazione della Biblia secundo il Muselmani', in *Bessarione* 38 (1926), 64–111 and 223–60.

36 See, for example, Qur'an 7:157 and 61:6. See also the important treatise of 'Ali b. Rabban al-Tabari, *al-Din wa al-Dawlah fi Ithbat Nubuwwat Muhammad*, trans. into English under the title *Religion and the Empire*.

37 See *Khutab wa Ahadith al-Qa'id al-Diniyah*, pp. 102–3.

38 *Ibid.*, p. 107.

39 *Ibid.*, p. 107.

40 *Ibid.*, pp. 103–4.

41 *Ibid.*, p. 100.

42 *al-Sijill al-Qawmi*, vol. 9, pp. 751–2.

43 Qur'an 3:63.

44 Qur'an 5:84.

45 Qur'an 7:159.

46 Qur'an 5:53.

47 *al-Kitab al-Akhdar*, part 1, p. 55.

48 Qur'an 41:42.

49 Qur'an 17:9.

50 Mu'ammar al-Qadhdhafi, *al-Multaqa al-Fikri al-Awwal lil-Talabah al-'Arab al-Darisin bi-al-Jamahiriyah* (Tripoli, Manshurat al-Markaz al-'Alami li-Abhath al-Kitab al-Akhdar, 1982), p. 39.

51 *Khutab wa-Ahadith al-Qa'id al-Diniyah*, p. 136.

52 *al-Sijill al-Qawmi*, vol. 4, p. 96.

53 *Ibid.*, p. 96.

54 *Ibid.*, p. 539.

55 *Ibid.*, p. 542.
56 *Ibid.*, vol. 8, pp. 403–9.
57 Qur'an 68:4.
58 Qur'an 53:2–3.
59 Qur'an 59:7 and 8:24.
60 Qur'an 4:64.
61 Qur'an 18:105.
62 See *Khutab wa-Ahadith al-Qa'id al-Diniyah*, pp. 145–52; and *al-Sijill al-Qawmi*, vol. 9, pp. 460ff.
63 Qur'an 32:2. See also 7:203 and 10:109.
64 See *al-Sijill al-Qawmi*, vol. 9, pp. 484–90.
65 *Khutab wa-Ahadith al-Qa'id al-Diniyah*, pp. 214–15.
66 *Ibid.*, p. 219.
67 *Ibid.*, p. 229.
68 *Ibid.*, pp. 222–3.
69 *Ibid.*, p. 227.
70 *Ibid.*, p. 233. See also pp. 229–33.
71 *Ibid.*, p. 237.
72 Qur'an 70:24–5; see also 51:19.
73 *Khutab wa-Ahadith al-Qa'id al-Diniyah*, p. 11.
74 Qur'an 4:2 and 131.
75 *Khutab wa-Ahadith al-Qa'id al-Diniyah*, p. 246.
76 *Ibid.*, p. 247.
77 See Muhammad Rashid Rida, *Tafsir al-Manar*, 12 vols. (Beirut, Dar al-Ma'rifah, n.d.) vol. 4, pp. 344–64.
78 Qur'an 49:11.
79 *Khutab wa-Ahadith al-Qa'id al-Diniyah*, p. 254.
80 These are the three consecutive months of Dhu al-Qi'dah, Dhu al-Hijjah, and Muharram, and the seventh month of the year, Rajab.
81 See Qur'an 1:188 and *Khutab wa-Ahadith al-Qa'id al-Diniyah*, p. 250.
82 Qur'an 9:34.
83 *Khutab wa-Ahadith al-Qa'id al-Diniyah*, p. 252.
84 Qur'an 16:71.
85 *Khutab wa-Ahadith al-Qa'id al-Diniyah*, p. 256.
86 *Ibid.*, pp. 258–9.
87 Qur'an 42:35.
88 *al-Sijill al-Qawmi*, vol. 14, p. 34.
89 *Ibid.*, p. 36.
90 *Ibid.*, vol. 4 (1972–73), p. 18.
91 *Ibid.*, vol. 14 (1982–83), p. 892; see also pp. 891–2.
92 *Khutab wa-Ahadith al-Qa'id al-Diniyah*, pp. 263–4.
93 Qur'an 16:89.
94 *Khutab wa-Ahadith al-Qa'id al-Diniyah*, p. 266.
95 Qur'an 74:11–17.

96 The saying 'Work for your hereafter as though you were going to die tomorrow, and for your life in this world as though you were going to live forever' is attributed to 'Ali. Qadhdhafi, however, cites it here as a saying of the Prophet.

97 Qur'an 17:16. See *Khutab wa-Ahadith al-Qa'id al-Diniyah*, p. 267.

98 Qur'an 8:61.

99 *Khutab wa-Ahadith al-Qa'id al-Diniyah*, p. 270.

100 *Ibid.*, pp. 274–5.

101 See Qur'an 5:13 and 14.

102 Qur'an 3:110.

103 *Khutab wa-Ahadith al-Qa'id al-Diniyah*, p. 277.

104 See *al-Sijill al-Qawmi*, vol. 14, pp. 51–2.

105 *Ibid.*, vol. 10, p. 395.

106 *Ibid.*, p. 292.

107 *Ibid.*, vol. 10, pp. 394–6.

108 *Ibid.*, vol. 1, p. 110.

109 *Ibid.*, vol. 2, p. 37.

110 *Ibid.*, vol. 3, p. 23.

111 *Ibid.*, vol. 7, pp. 214–15.

112 *Ibid.*, p. 686.

113 *Ibid.*, vol. 4, pp. 445–56.

114 *Ibid.*, vol. 4, pp. 445–6.

115 *Ibid.*, vol. 14, pp. 621–3.

116 Salah al-Jibali, *Thawrat al-Fatih wa-al-Ishtirakiyah* (Tripoli, Maktabat al-Fikr, 1974), p. 13.

117 Qur'an 57:7.

118 Quoted in Salah al-Jibali, p. 19; see also pp. 15–23.

119 Bukhari, *Sahih, Bab al-Harth*.

120 Qur'an 6:132.

121 Ibn Maja, *Sunan, Bab al-Ruhun*.

122 Qur'an 49:13.

123 al-Tirmidhi, *al-Jami' al-Sahih, Bab Tafsir Surat al-Hujurat*.

124 Qur'an 2:177 and 245.

125 Muslim, *Sahih, Bab al-Nikah*.

126 Qur'an 2:143.

127 Qur'an 5:2.

128 *al-Sijill al-Qawmi*, vol. 6, pp. 174–5.

4
Qadhdhafi's Ideology

The mover of human history is the social or ethnic factor.
There is no real rival to the social factor in influencing the
unity of any one given social group except the religious
factor, which can divide a single ethnic society, and which is
capable of uniting diverse social groups with disparate
ethnic identities. In the end, however, the social factor
prevails.[1]

In *The Green Book* Qadhdhafi is addressing an essentially non-
Muslim audience. There the subjects of religion and national
identity are treated so broadly and simply that many questions are
left unanswered. The various currents of nationalism in Europe and
their influence on movements in the Near East, and the diverse
approaches which the latter have taken to religion, are some of the
issues which must at least be noted. It is, however, with the issue of
the conflict of Islamic and national identity, or the possible harmony
between the two, that the present discussion will be concerned.

In the West the dictum 'Render therefore to Caesar the things
that are Caesar's, and to God the things that are God's' was realized
finally in the separation of church and state. Yet since Islam began
as a socio-political order in which everything, including Caesar,
belongs to God, the *ummah* becomes at one and the same time both
church and state. It is the tension between a strictly Islamic or a
strictly ethnic or national identity which has occupied both Islamic
revivalists and nationalistic movements throughout the world of
Islam in modern history.

Qadhdhafi's ideas on nationalism and religion as the two essential
frameworks within which human history moves were, although

original, not born in a vacuum. They are a synthesis of a long process of Islamic thought both in North Africa and the Arab East. It may be generally argued that in North Africa the dominant problem was not that of nationalism, but Islamic identity. This was not because the Muslim thinkers of North Africa had any doubt regarding their faith commitment to Islam, but rather because they were responding to a Christian European colonialist endeavour which aimed at destroying their faith as well as their national identity. Qadhdhafi is heir to Muslim activists such as the early founders of the Sanusiyah order in Libya, and to later religiously motivated fighters (*mujahidin*) such as 'Umar al-Mukhtar, Ahmad al-Sharif, and other national heroes who resisted Italian occupation. He is also heir to both the religious and national movements which struggled against French colonialism in the rest of North Africa, notably the heroes of the Algerian revolution.

The main currents of religious reform and Arab nationalism, however, emerged in the eastern provinces of the Ottoman Empire in the nineteenth century as a result of the interaction between Arab-Islamic thought and Western thought and education. Nor were only Muslims involved in discussing Arab nationalism and its relationship to Islam as a faith and civilization; Christian thinkers also played an important role in the growth and crystallization of this ideology. While there is no evidence that Qadhdhafi was directly influenced by these currents, it is important to discuss these developments in order to place his ideas in their proper historical context. The need and problems behind the call for religious reform and nationalist revival in the nineteenth century remain essentially valid for the Arab world today. It is not surprising, therefore, to see many similarities and coincidences of thought between Qadhdhafi and earlier Arab-Islamic thinkers.

It has been observed that 'As a symbol of unity and identity, Islam is to North Africa what Arab nationalism is to the Arab East'.[2] This, of course, is an overstatement. Nevertheless, it can hardly be denied that the struggle of the Maghrib or Western lands of the Arab world against colonialism and cultural and religious disintegration was led by and large by the *ulama'*, Sufi shaykhs, and other comn.itted Muslim activists. North African history in this sense, however, has helped to form Qadhdhafi's character rather than his thought. His commitment to Islam is no more due to his North African environment than that of a Turk, Yugoslav or North American is due to his particular environment. It is therefore best to leave aside the particular Islam of North Africa for the present. It is to the thinkers of Egypt and Syria that we must turn, where the proper context of Qadhdhafi's religious ideas may be found.

As the process of the decline and final demise of the Ottoman Empire escalated, many of its subjects, Muslims and non-Muslims, began to look for ways of asserting their own distinct cultural and national identities. But the Ottoman Empire was an Islamic state which defended Islam and had enlarged its domains for centuries. The first and natural reaction of Muslim thinkers was to call for a pan-Islamic movement which could galvanize Muslims everywhere for the struggle against the colonialist ambitions of European powers. Among the greatest champions of the pan-Islamic movement in the Arab world was Muhammad 'Abduh (1849–1905). Muhammad 'Abduh was less of a political activist than his mentor, Jamal al-Din al-Afghani; he was, rather, a reformer. He lived in a society with a Muslim majority and a small but active Coptic Christian minority. He was thus directly involved in the religious pluralism which has been so characteristic of Egypt and the Arab east from time immemorial.

'Abduh spoke with enthusiasm and nostalgia of the past power and glory of the Islamic caliphate. He wrote the following words in 1886 from his exile in Beirut to the Shaykh al-Islam (chief religious authority) in Istanbul:

> The Islamic caliphate is like a high wall and a fortress. But the strongest of its walls is the trust which the hearts of the people of faith possess in it, and their valor in defending it. There is no motivation for trust or power to rekindle valor in the hearts of Muslims, except in what religion provides for them. Thus anyone who thinks that the name of the fatherland, national interest or any such high-sounding slogans can take the place of religion in raising the ardor of the people and directing it to the desired end, has no doubt strayed from the right way.[3]

Elsewhere 'Abduh has insisted on the necessity for the people of every country to unite and work together for the common good, in spite of their religious differences. He also advocated complete religious freedom and social equality for all citizens. Still he felt that only a strong, confident and dynamic Muslim state could guarantee such freedom for both Muslims and non-Muslims. He therefore called on all Muslims to unite in order for them to recreate that golden age of the 'righteous forebears', which he did not limit to the time of the first four 'rightly-guided' caliphs, but extended over the first three centuries of Muslim history. In this he echoed the ideas of Afghani who had earlier called for unity and cooperation among all the people of the East against Western colonialism.[4]

Muhammad 'Abduh's disciple and successor, Muhammad Rashid Rida (d. 1935), grew up in Syria, where religious pluralism is far more pronounced than in Egypt. In a fiery address delivered in September 1932 on the occasion of the remembrance of Salah al-Din (Saladdin) and his famous Battle of Hittin against the forces of the Crusaders, Rida called on all Arabs to support both an Arab and Islamic unity. This he saw as the only way towards strength and progress of a nation which had once led the world in science and technology and in religious and social tolerance. Rida argued that when the Arabs had lost power in Muslim society, Islam itself as a single religious system was fragmented, and with it the Muslim *ummah*. He called on the Arabs of his time to be guided by the example of Salah al-Din in valour and magnanimity, but above all in his relentless *jihad* for the liberation of the holy city of Jerusalem from the Franks, for both Muslims and Christians. Rida called for a religious and patriotic *jihad* to regain and preserve the power and dignity of the Arab nation.[5]

Rashid Rida's synthesis of Arab nationalism and Islamic unity has been shared by a number of both Muslim and Christian intellectuals. Among Muslim thinkers Shakib Arslan, a member of a noted Druze family and himself descended from the famous Arab Tanukhi tribe, spent his long intellectual career analyzing and defending the Islamic world and its heritage. Shakib Arslan (1869–1946) witnessed the turmoil which accompanied the dismemberment of the Ottoman Islamic state, the Arab awakening and the ensuing Arab bitterness against Western betrayal and outright colonization of the Arab world. Portraying the gloomy condition of the Islamic world at the time, Arslan asked the persistent question, 'Why have the Muslims fallen behind the rest of the civilized world?'[6]

Nadrah Matran, a Syrian Christian who also lived during this period of Arab awakening and disappointment, advocated in 1913 Arabism as a cultural and linguistic identity for all Arabs, regardless of their religious affiliations. He noted with approval the support of the Syrian Arabs of the Ghassanid Christian tribe for their Muslim

Arab 'brothers' in their conquest of Damascus. Matran saw Islam as the basis of an Arab glory which had to be preserved at all costs – even, if necessary, the rule of the Saljuks who were non-Arab Muslims. A Syrian Christian contemporary of Matran expressed this nationalistic sentiment most succinctly: 'Let everyone say I am Arab . . . and if being Arab is only possible through being Muslim, then let him say I am an Arab and a Muslim.'[7]

The purpose of the preceding brief discussion is not to suggest that Colonel Qadhdhafi brought nothing new to the long debate among Arab thinkers on their identity, and hence their heritage and destiny, but rather to demonstrate that his concerns have been voiced by many before him, and no doubt will continue to be voiced so long as the dream of Arab unity remains a dream and not a reality. Qadhdhafi, as has been made amply clear in this study, remains committed to the realization of his dream at all costs. It is this hope which underlies his faith and vision, and constitutes the fundamental framework of his ideology.

Religion and Nationalism as Movers of History

It has been commonly held that Qadhdhafi is the disciple and immediate successor of Gamel Nasser, the champion of Arab unity and of Arabism as a powerful symbol of national pride. There is no doubt that Qadhdhafi, like most Arabs at the height of Nasser's popularity, were inspired by a man who rekindled a sense of unity, self-worth and dignity among the Arabs as no one had done before. Still Qadhdhafi, we believe, differs sharply in several respects from his mentor. Nasser's socialist ideas were far more traditional than those of Qadhdhafi, who has insisted on the Islamic basis of a new and all-encompassing philosophy. Nasser, as has already been observed, saw Islam as a useful 'circle' within which Arabs and non-Arabs could move in their effort to build a strong non-allied movement representing millions of Asian and African Muslims. For Qadhdhafi, Islam is the fundamental basis of Arab identity, of unity within the Arab nation and between it and all Muslims. It is the most effective political and cultural weapon against Western imperialism and cultural hegemony.

The Arab-Islamic synthesis of Rashid Rida and other thinkers had unfortunately given way to nationalist movements which have only paid lip service to religion and to Islam. Thus, in his address to the second conference of the Islamic Call Society, to which reference has already been made, Qadhdhafi sharply criticized the slogan of the Syrian Ba'th Party: 'God and revolution can never meet.' He asserted that *al-fatih* revolution is unique because it is at once Islamic and socialist. He continued: 'We are now about to see the results of this crucial thesis. We are now at the end of a stage which has enabled us to derive the necessary lessons from the past and its serious endeavours.'[8] The endeavours of which Qadhdhafi spoke were those which aimed at defining the religious and nationalist personality of the Arab people and plotting a course of action that would enable them to realize this personality in all its dimensions. Among the most important lessons of the past is the realization that Western models of nationalism without religion are not only foreign, but deleterious to both the Arab and Muslim identity.

Although religion is necessary to provide a perennial source of guidance in society, nationhood or ethnic identity provides the social structure within which religion can operate. Thus Qadhdhafi has argued: 'Ethnic identity (*qawmiyah*) is a natural and real *a priori* social principle whose function is to bind together the people of a community even before they have a religion.'[9] None the less, religion and nationalism have been instrumental in all the major currents of history. They may at times act together, or separately, or even at odds with one another, depending on the conflicting demands of loyalty which each may require of the same community. It is necessary, Qadhdhafi believes, that nationalism be respected and religion be held as sacred – not only Islam and Arab nationalism, but nationalism and religion as abstract principles. Qadhdhafi stated this belief in a symposium which the French newspaper *Le Monde* organized in Paris in November 1973. He argued further in that symposium that the authenticity of a nation's character can only be achieved by returning to the roots, to the authentic source of that nation's culture and history. Renewal of positive change in a society can only be achieved by the self-re-evaluation of a society's history, and particularly the events and developments which led to wars and conflicts.[10]

One of the popular slogans of the Nasser era was 'Religion belongs to God, and the fatherland belongs to all'. This meant that religion should not be made the cause of national conflicts among different religious groups. It was also interpreted to mean that religion is simply a private affair which must be completely separated from state politics. This was carried even further by the late Anwar Sadat, who declared: 'No politics in religion, or religion in politics'. This in fact means a sort of Islamic separation of church and state. Qadhdhafi has always insisted, as can be surmised from our discussion thus far, that Islam and politics cannot be separated.

Qadhdhafi is aware of this difference with Nasser. He asserted in an interview with the leftist Lebanese newspaper *al-Safir*, held in January 1975, that Nasserism is not a stagnant tradition (*sunnah*), nor would he accept it as such. The interviewer then asked Colonel Qadhdhafi about the separation of religion and state affairs. He replied that this idea may apply to other religions, but not to Islam because Islam covers all aspects of life. The Qur'an itself presents legislation which would apply to all the major issues of life. Islam, he further argued, is not only a religion of rites and rituals. 'I believe', he went on, 'that separation of religion and state is a contrived act in this situation. I say that separating the Islamic religion from the state is an arbitrary decision and is practically impossible. Religion is one and all-encompassing.' He then cited the Qur'anic words, 'Surely the religion with God is Islam.'[11] The interviewer protested that most Arab rulers and thinkers would not agree with Qadhdhafi's point of view. But Qadhdhafi countered: 'We shall continue to dialogue with those who do not agree until they become convinced.'[12]

It was observed earlier in this discussion that Qadhdhafi regards Islam as a faith and cultural heritage, as the only weapon against imperialism and intellectual domination. It must be stressed, however, that he displays unwavering faith in this heritage and its great and universal values, not simply as a political instrument but in itself. On the admission of Somalia into the Arab League (2 March 1974), Qadhdhafi addressed a popular rally in the capital Mogadishu. His statements are highly instructive. He observed that there are definite attempts by both world communism and Western imperialism to create doubts in the minds of the Arab and Islamic peoples concerning their religion and civilization, and even in their capacity to catch up with the modern age without help from either of the two camps. He went on: 'I wish to alert us all to the fact that neocolonialism is trying in one way or another to stand between us and our efforts to revitalize our past and heritage, which would help us in plotting our course for the future. We must be eager to preserve our values which are our religion and history, and which can be our strong weapon in the battle of life.' Qadhdhafi further observed that both the East and West consider Arabs as primitive tribes in need of teachers in communism and capitalism. 'But we shall make our future ourselves with the free will of our peoples. Prophets came out of these deserts, and they were Bedouins. We were the first to advocate human rights when 'Umar (the second Caliph) protested: "How can you enslave human beings when their mothers gave birth to them as free beings?" '[13]

In February 1975, Qadhdhafi was asked his opinion by the Kuwaiti magazine *Majallat al-Ra'id* of the extent to which the Arab people should allow themselves to be influenced by outside intellectual currents. He counselled: 'We should first recover our identity and our Arab intellectual heritage; then we will be able to interact with the rest of the world and listen to what it has to say to us. This is because we would then be able to give as well. But this will not be achieved until we are able to stand on our own feet.'[14]

In answer to another question regarding the role of religious education in building the personality of the Arab individual, Qadhdhafi said: 'There is no life without religion! We find that even those who do not believe in one of the "heavenly religions", still adopt a "positive" or man-made religion. It is noteworthy that Muslims have allowed themselves to be fully engrossed in this subject, which we debate as though it has nothing to do with our faith, or as if faith is not necessary. If we accept this thesis, then we would be the only atheists in the world. This is because those who spread such ideas among us, themselves have their own religious beliefs. Even avowed atheists have their beliefs, whatever their nature may be.'[15]

It must have become evident from our discussion thus far that Qadhdhafi is an idealist. He has called, as we saw above, for the respect of religion and nationalism even as abstract principles. Here he expresses the obvious fact that 'were relations of mutual respect for the integrity of all national and religious identities to be established among the nations of the world, then all hostilities and conflicts would cease'. 'Of course', Colonel Qadhdhafi added, 'this would be the ideal situation, but unfortunately the inevitable reality is that this struggle shall continue among religions and nationalisms.'[16] But, it may be asked, is it not this struggle which has given both religion and nationalism such a primary role in human history?

The Arab Nation: Its Role and Mission

It has been repeatedly emphasized that an important aspect of Qadhdhafi's religious as well as his nationalist ideology is his vision of Arab unity. This vision has been shared by many Arabs, both Muslims and Christians. But for him it has been a practical imperative which takes precedence over all sectarian and interreligious considerations. Qadhdhafi finds support for this imperative in the 'Divine conception' of Islam, as discussed in the previous chapter. Religion thus conceived is more important than ethnic identity, although nationalist, or ethnic, identity historically predates religion.

For many Arab nationalist thinkers, the Arab people are a single nation. But while for most contemporary thinkers religion is to be ignored, or at least subordinated to Arabism, for Qadhdhafi religion is an integral part of Arab identity. For many, religion is a divisive factor; for Qadhdhafi it is a uniting force. He expresses this idea somewhat bluntly as follows: 'In short, we cannot prefer the role or status of a non-Christian over that of a Christian. This is because it is the cause of Arab nationalism which is at issue, so long as we are within the Arab fatherland.' Even the problem of religious freedom would cease to be a problem, Qadhdhafi asserts, 'if we accept the "Divine conception" of Islam. That is if we recognize the One God, and realize that we all are followers of the prophets, and that we are all *muslims* to God.'[17]

Qadhdhafi carries this tolerant attitude further to include even those who worship idols. He cites the Qur'anic verse: 'If one of the Associators seeks refuge with you, grant him refuge in order that he may hear the word of God; then bring him safely to his own place of security.'[18] 'This means in our life in the modern world', Qadhdhafi commented, 'that if there is a group of our people who share with us a common fatherland, should we persecute them and not grant them their rights? No, rather we should give them protection and answer their cries for help. We should call them to the truth, and not to the sword! This call to the truth means that we should establish dialogue, debate and discussion with them. This may lead to some positive influence on their beliefs, and thus they may become Muslims like us. We and they should arrive at a specific agreement that no harm should come from either of our groups to the other.'[19]

It was observed in the first chapter of this study that one of the first priorities of the revolution of 1 September was to work for the achievement of Arab unity. This was conceived not simply as a symbolic unity of purpose and identity, but as the eventual merger of all Arab countries into one single state or federation. That this goal has not been attained, Qadhdhafi believes, is due to the machinations of world imperialism. He thus observed: 'Colonialism wishes to hinder the progress towards achieving a complete union. It wishes to hinder the unity of all Arab republics, and Arab unity in general. Thus it has begun to disseminate false propaganda against the 1 September Revolution. Yet the only accusation it could bring against the Revolution is that it has raised the banner of Islam. It then asks, "What future will this bring to Christians in Arab lands"?' Qadhdhafi countered this accusation by saying: 'The First of September Revolution has raised the banner of Islam in accordance with the Qur'an, in accordance with the principle of *islam* [submission] to God which regards anyone who has faith in God, His Books and Messengers, to be a Muslim.'[20]

We have already noted Colonel Qadhdhafi's strong aversion to any form of party organization in an Arab and Muslim society 'of the masses'. In a meeting with a group of law students on 28 April 1973, the Leader considered party politics to be a crime against religion. He declared: 'The great party is the entire people, and the religion is the Islamic faith. We cannot', he continued, 'transform this universal religion into a party, or empty noises in the dark.'[21] Qadhdhafi has in mind the Muslim Brothers and the Party of Islamic Liberation (*Hizb al-Tahrir al-Islami*), both of which he considers to be serving the interests of Western imperialism. He rejects the idea of spreading Islam from Europe, rather than its natural grounds which are the minarets and pulpits of the mosques.

In an interview given in February 1973 to a Lebanese journalist from the newspaper *al-Bayraq*, Qadhdhafi emphatically declared, in answer to a question concerning the activities of the Muslim Brothers in Libya, 'We reject that Islam, which is a universal religion, be turned into empty clatter, secret cells and other such activities in the dark. Let all the people of faith come out to the street and declare their faith with ringing voices! As for discussion of the Muslim Brothers, we even refuse to talk about them.' Qadhdhafi then told the journalist that for four years an opportunity had been given to all party affiliates to come out and debate their views. Since no one had responded to its invitation, anyone now who carries out any party activities, be it the Muslim Brothers or any other party, would be severely punished. This is because the purpose of such a person would be not social or religious reform, but the usurpation of popular authority under the guise of a religious party.[22]

In an important pamphlet which presents clearly Mu'ammar al-Qadhdhafi's thought and even style, if not his words,[23] the nature, role and mission of the Arab nation are set forth with great force and lucidity. The author asserts: 'The relationship between the Arab nation as an ethnic identity and Islam as a message intended for humankind is a close organic relationship. It is the Arab nation which has borne the Islamic message, and which its sons carried to all the peoples the support for this organic unity between Arab nationalism and Islam in both the life of the Prophet and the Qur'an.'[24] The Prophet was, he believes, both a nationalist leader through his sublime example, and he was the Messenger of God to humanity in the good example of his life. He was so happy with his Arab identity that he thanked God for providentially allowing him to be born on the day on which God preserved the dignity and honour of the Arabs and granted them victory over their enemies.[25] The Prophet loved his people and did not love those who despise them. The author relates that the Prophet one day said to Salman the Persian, 'Do not despise me lest you abandon your faith!' Salman replied: 'How can I despise you when through you God guided us!' The Prophet said 'If you despise the Arabs, you despise me.' The author relates still another *hadith* on the authority of 'Uthman (the third caliph), who heard the Prophet say: 'Anyone who deceives the Arabs will not be included in my intercession, nor will he attain my friendship.'[26]

The author's arguments from the Qur'an rely first on those verses which speak of the Qur'an as an Arabic revelation,[27] and second on the verses which speak of the *ummah* and *qawm*, which constituted the society of the first Muslims. Third, the author finds in the Qur'anic verses which speak of the obligations of every Muslim towards his or her next of kin yet another instance of support of the notion of ethnic identity, or *qawmiyah*.[28] Since, however, Colonel Qadhdhafi has himself discussed a number of such verses, we shall base our discussion directly on his remarks concerning this important matter.

Colonel Qadhdhafi begins his discussion of the Qur'anic basis of Arab nationalism with another important Qur'anic concept, namely the diversity of cultures, languages, colours and religions in human society.[29] He says: 'Anyone who despises a black person, for instance, or one who speaks a different language from his own, is in the wrong.' Islam has from its beginning upheld the principles of universality and internationalism. Qadhdhafi, however, adds: 'Yet at the same time, Islam did not destroy ethnic identities. This is because in destroying ethnic identities one destroys the entire *ummah* [community of Islam]. The world is made up of different communities; thus destroying a community is like destroying one of the world-families, from the viewpoint of the rest of the world communities.' Qadhdhafi then cites the Qur'anic verse: 'Give to the next of kin his due', and comments: 'The Qur'an, therefore, commands us to prefer the nearest of kin in giving assistance. The nearest of kin with regard to us are the Arab peoples who must come before the Persian peoples, for example, in spite of the fact that both are Muslims. There is no question but that we must stand with the Arabs and assist them because they are of our own ethnic identity [*qawmiyah*].' Then, directly addressing his people, the Leader said: 'It is better for you that you assist your near relations, whether this relationship be that of blood, the family, tribe, or even a social relationship. But it is necessary that this bias in favor of close relations be in quest of good, not evil ends.' The Arab nation, Qadhdhafi counsels, must first achieve internal unity before it can provide effective assistance to other Muslim nations.[30]

Qadhdhafi's belief in the potential and the ultimate destiny of the Arab nation, and in the value of its religion as an essential component of its greatness, remains firm. The following remarks made at the opening session of the first conference of the Arab Socialist Union, in March 1972, reflect admirably this unwavering faith. The conference was held in Cairo after Nasser's death and more than a decade of the dissolution of the Syro-Egyptian union. Qadhdhafi said: 'However bitter the reality of the Arab nation may be at present, still it is the nation most fit to lead first itself, and then the Third World. It is still capable of offering much to humankind.' This is because the Arab nation has special characteristics which other nations do not have: 'The Arab nation has special spiritual, material and strategic characteristics. Its earth has been the ground of civilizations, and its heaven the heaven of revelation. The entire world needs the Arab nation, but we do not need to import ideas from the East or West as others do.'[31]

Addressing a large gathering in Tripoli in September 1972, Qadhdhafi insisted that nationalism is not a return to the time of *jahiliyah*, the time of foolishness and ignorance before Islam. In this he was answering the charge of the Muslim Brothers who regard any nationalistic sentiment as a recurrence of pre-Islamic blood solidarity (*asabiyah*) among the Arab tribes which should be replaced by the brotherhood of faith. Yet Qadhdhafi argues, again from the Qur'an, for Arab nationalism. Citing once more the injunction, 'Give the next of kin his due', he comments, 'it is as though God says "You must preserve the integrity of the family, tribe, people and the nation". That is to say, blood kinship [*silat al-rahim*] or kinship ties are sacred.' He argues further that the nation is in reality one enlarged family. Thus kinship is graduated: the nearest being that of the parents.[32]

Qadhdhafi goes further in support of his ideology to argue that the Qur'anic verse, 'You are the best community given to humankind',[33] refers to the Arab nation. 'The meaning of this verse is clear', Qadhdhafi asserted, 'it is the Arab *ummah*. The Arab nation is the *ummah* and the communities around it are "the people" [*nas*] to whom it was given.'[34]

It must be observed that in as much as the first Muslims to whom the verse was primarily addressed were predominantly Arabs, Qadhdhafi's interpretation is correct. He insisted in the same speech that without Islam, the Arab nation would have become extinct: 'Had it not been for this Divine message, the Arabs would not have been a unified society, or a nation.' In support of this assertion, Qadhdhafi again cites a verse of the Qur'an.[35]

The verse under discussion, it should be noted, is not an unconditional statement. Rather, it goes on to say: 'You enjoin the good, forbid evil and have faith in God.' Only when these conditions are realized does the *ummah*, whether it is the larger Muslim *ummah* or the Arab nation, merit the honour of being 'the best community given to humankind'. It is most probable that Colonel Qadhdhafi intended by these remarks to strengthen Arab unity, as he also said, 'Fragmentation means death.' But if this idea is to be taken literally and applied to the Arab people of every age, then it may lead to the notion of a 'chosen people'. This notion is dangerous, no matter how noble its purpose may be.

Colonel Qadhdhafi also refers the verse: 'Thus have we made you a community of the middle course, in order that you may be witnesses over humankind'[36] to the Arab nation. He said: 'You are this *ummah* which shall bear witness over the people who enter into Islam.' Again, the verse goes on to say, 'and the Messenger shall be a witness over you'. The verse, according to the *tafsir* (literature of commentary on the Qur'an) classical and contemporary, refers to the Day of Judgement when the Muslim community will bear witness that all the prophets of God delivered His messages to their communities.[37] Colonel Qadhdhafi himself admits the novelty of his ideas. He said: 'I can say that I have never heard such words before, even though they are in the Qur'an [that is, "I admit that my interpretation is unique."]'[38]

It may thus seem that Qadhdhafi places the values of 'Arabism' above those of 'Islamism'. A synthesis of his thought would more aptly suggest, however, that Arabism and Islamism are, for Qadhdhafi, inseparable, each one being necessary for the realization of the other. At times he goes even further, identifying Arabism with Islam. On 8 March 1979 in an 'historic proclamation' given at a meeting of the Revolutionary Committees, Qadhdhafi argued that 'It is not possible to separate the revival of Arab nationalism from the revival of the Arab Islamic identity'. This is a fact which history has painfully proven, at least since 1948 and the establishment of a Jewish state in the heart of the Arab world. Colonel Qadhdhafi, however, drew a different conclusion from this point. He continued: 'For one to be an Arab and not a Muslim: this is something not intended by the Muhammadan message. It is possible that the punishment of such a person on the Day of Judgement shall be specifically severe. That one could be a Muslim without being an Arab: this too was not first intended. Thus the reward of such a person on the Last Day shall be manifold.' Qadhdhafi goes on to assert: 'Islam is the religion of the Arab nation. Muhammad is the prophet of the Arabs, and the Qur'an is the scripture of the Arabs.'[39]

Colonel Qadhdhafi cites a number of Qur'anic verses in support of this idea. These are verses which speak of the Qur'an as an Arabic scripture, one of which is especially noteworthy. It reads, 'Thus have We sent down to you an Arabic Qur'an in order that you may warn the Mother of the Cities [Makkah] and those who are around it.'[40] This is a Makkan verse which was later superseded by such declarations as 'We have not sent you except as a mercy to humankind' and 'We have surely sent you to all human beings as a bearer of glad tidings and a warner.'[41] Colonel Qadhdhafi has on many occasions, as we have seen, argued for the universality of both the Qur'an and the mission of the Prophet Muhammad. The only reasonable explanation of the statements under discussion, therefore, is that his intent here is to stress the close and organic relation-ship of the Arabic language, culture and identity with Islam. There is no doubt but that Arabs have a special role to play in the continued growth and propagation of Islam, whose language of worship, law and theology is Arabic. Thus in spite of the growth of a rich non-Arabic Islamic literature, Arabic, the language of the Qur'an, of the Prophetic *sunnah* and of classical Muslim civilization, remains the only vehicle through which Islam can authentically express itself.

An important question, however, remains: who are the Arabs? Is Arab identity simply an ethnic or blood relation, or is it also an historic, cultural and linguistic identity, and a shared destiny? Mu'ammar al-Qadhdhafi would include all these elements in his definition of Arab identity. But sometimes he stresses one and at other times another of its dimensions. In November 1974, in the final session of the Arab Socialist Union convention, he declared: 'Arab identity [*al-'urubah*] is not one of origin, nor blood relation. Rather it is one of affiliation, from the Atlantic to the Gulf.'[42]

Colonel Qadhdhafi is not an armchair philosopher. He expresses his views in extemporized speeches dictated by the occasion on which each is to be delivered. While his main purpose, and even the logic supporting it, is clear and constant throughout, his emphases may often vary. His approach to social and religious issues is fun-damental and direct. Inconsistencies, where they occur, pertain to non-essential matters.

There is no doubt that for Mu'ammar al-Qadhdhafi, a strong Arab nation, aware of its history and mission, is necessary for a meaningful and vibrant Islamic identity. Yet the question remains as to how a balance can be maintained between the Islamic and ethnic dimensions of such an identity. How should the Arab nation, striving for unity, treat its non-Arab Muslim minorities? A sym-pathetic Arab writer, reflecting on Qadhdhafi's views of Islam and Arab nationalism, offers the following wise counsel:

We must not let our radios loudly sing the praises of Arabs and Arabism day and night, while there are among us the Kurd, Turk and Pakistani. We must be aware of our status before our Lord. So long as we abide by Islam as our faith, we should not boast before others, especially if we and they are citizens of one state. In this way we will be able to avoid raising the spectres of ethnocentrism ['*asabiyah*] and atheism. We must strive always to preserve our unique status, if we are to ensure our very existence and strength. It is only then that we will have the power to guarantee for Islam security and power.[43]

In a social philosophy based on the principles of social justice, equality and freedom, the fate of the 'Kurd and the Turk' as members of national minorities in the 'new society' is an important issue which calls for some comment. Qadhdhafi is not unaware of these problems; it is to the solutions proposed by his political and religious theories that we now turn.

Religion and Nationalism: the Problem of Minorities

Colonel Qadhdhafi, as we saw earlier in this study,[44] recognizes only two kinds of minorities in society. The first is a minority which belongs to a specific national entity, such as the Kurds and Armenians. The second are simply political, or religious minorities without a national base, such as the Gypsies and Jews. Members of national minorities, wherever they may be scattered among various nation-states, retain common national aspirations and a shared destiny. The religious factor remains always subordinate to the nationalist identity in such minorities. Political minorities, however, have neither national rights nor patriotic claims. Their social, political, religious and economic rights must be guaranteed by society.

Unlike other eastern Arab countries, Libya has a religiously homogeneous society. Its single ethnic minority is, at present, the Berbers who have their own traditional language but who share the religion, history, culture and even language of their Arab compatriots. The Berbers, therefore, constitute neither a religious nor a national minority, but a political problem, largely created by European colonialism.

Coming from this very background, Colonel Qadhdhafi considers all minorities to be simply social groups, whose equality and full participation in society must be safeguarded. In other words, Qadhdhafi does not accept the notion that a minority can lay claims to a separate state or nationhood simply on the basis of its distinct religious identity. Even the religious rights of such a minority are in reality political and social rights, and should be treated as such.

Addressing a group of young intellectuals in the Mauritanian capital, Nouakchott, (23 July 1983), Qadhdhafi insisted that minorities should be given their independence, in order that no excesses against the national identity of a country be committed in the interest of religion. He further argued, 'It is indeed a serious matter if we begin to favor claims of ethnic and cultural superiority [*shu'ubiyah*] at the expense of Arab nationalism. This is because that is exactly what imperialism wishes us to do.' He then declared: 'I do not believe in the domination of Arab nationalism over any other national identity.' He further believes that minorities like the Kurds, Armenians and blacks should be allowed to secede from their countries and form their own states. [45]

We saw in Chapter 2 that Colonel Qadhdhafi gives priority to the nationalist factor over the religious one in the growth of nationalistic societies. He remarked that during the Abbasid period, Arabs and Persians shared a common identity, and during the Ottoman period the Arabs and Turks constituted one single state. But in the end, Persians and Turks asserted their own national identity. Arabs also recovered their own national identity, and after a long struggle achieved their national independence. From this, it is clear that Qadhdhafi does not believe in the viability of a pan-Islamic state. Rather, the ideal is that national Muslim states should cooperate, but at the same time each should maintain its own ethnic character. Not only Arabs, but all the nationalities included in the Ottoman Empire, including Turks, were justified in seceding and forming their own national entities. Yet, he protests, 'Many accused us [Arabs] of being seceders, advocates of cultural superiority [*shu'ubiyah*], unbelievers, and against the Caliph. Multitudes of martyrs fell in defense of such empty notions.' But, he retorted, 'We were not seceders, nor were we ethnocentric, or unbelievers! Rather we were an Arab nation wishing to be independent from the Turkish nation.' Then, echoing *The Green Book*, Colonel Qadhdhafi concluded: 'Thus in the end, it is always the nationalist factor which prevails.' [46]

It was observed in our discussion of the third part of *The Green Book* that Colonel Qadhdhafi holds that every ethnic group or nation must have their own religion. In December 1980, an international symposium on Mu'ammar al-Qadhdhafi's thought in *The Green Book* was held at the Free University of Madrid. In that symposium Colonel Qadhdhafi discussed certain groups in society which he considers to be oppressed. Among the groups discussed at some length were minorities. He reiterated his assertion in *The Green Book* that every people must have their own religious tradition and character. In Madrid, he argued that the only legitimate minority is a nationalist minority. Scientifically speaking, there is no religious minority. Anyone who embraces a religion other than the religion of his own people would be doing the wrong thing. Every ethnic group should be embodied in a nation, and every nation should have its own faith. Hence, any group of people which embraces a religion other than the religion of their own people would forfeit any national rights and duties because their action would be fundamentally unsound. By religion Qadhdhafi means not simply a religious tradition, but an ideology, including atheism.[47]

This seemingly controversial view of religion and nationality is actually a traditional Islamic view. The word *'millah'* as used in the Qur'an and later tradition means 'faith community'. It came to designate the religious communities which lived under Islamic rule. These were recognized, and for the most part exercised their religious and cultural heritage freely. Qadhdhafi has in mind not the long and formative history of such faith communities, but the recent movements which led to many political and social problems within the Arab and Muslim communities. The Ahmadiyah movement in India and later Pakistan, and the Babi and Bahai in Iran, are three cases in point.

In the Arab world in particular, Christian communities, and especially those allied with the Protestant or Catholic West, have been uncertain of their national and religious loyalties. This only led to mistrust and suspicion among communities which share a common history, culture and destiny. Qadhdhafi, moreover, regards all Arabs, regardless of their religious affiliation, as one people belonging to the great Arab-Islamic civilization. It is for this reason that he insists on regarding them all as Muslims. Nor was he alone in this view, as we have already seen.

A unique community – religiously, culturally and even ethnically – with which Qadhdhafi has been concerned, deserves some attention. The Jewish community is not only unique, but crucially important to the Arab world today. He emphatically declared at the Madrid symposium: 'The Jews cannot be regarded as a minority. A French Jew, for example, has no right to migrate to Palestine, because his true home is France and his nationality is French. The migration of Jews from their national homes to Palestine, and building there a colonial and racist new society, led to the Middle East problem. It will no doubt eventually lead to a third world war.' Qadhdhafi believes that the Jews are not an ethnic minority such as the Kurds and Armenians. He thus invited the Libyan Jews to return from Europe to their original country, Libya, where they would live like all other Libyans. He said: 'I wish to extend on this occasion a warm welcome to all Libyan Jews back to Libya, and I would myself undertake to guarantee them absolute equality in the "new and free society of the masses". They will be equal in all rights and obligations with all other Libyans. They will also be able to practice their faith in their homes and places of worship in full liberty.'[48]

Qadhdhafi was not making empty promises. Rather, he was reiterating one of the basic principles of his Third Universal Theory. He thus explained that only the 'new society of the masses' can offer a final and just solution to the problem of minorities because it ensures the equality of all its members in the distribution of wealth and authority. A minority does not normally fight for a language or social customs, but rather for economic and political rights. Since the 'society of the masses' has no wage-earners or exploitation of any kind, there is then no reason for minority revolts.[49]

Returning to the Jewish question, Qadhdhafi invited all Arab Jews to return to their original Arab homes. He again stressed:

> Scientifically and analytically, Arab Jews do not constitute a
> minority in the Arab World. Oriental Jews (that is
> Sephardic Jews) are the 'Children of Israel'. They thus
> constitute a particular ethnic entity distinct from that of the
> Arabs. They have the right to live in Palestine. As for those
> who migrated to Palestine just because they are Jews, they
> should return to their countries of origin. There is no
> justification for them to occupy Palestine.[50]

Qadhdhafi may seem, from the picture we have presented in this study, as an impractical idealist. That he is an idealist is a fact that can hardly be contested. But he is not, in our view, an impractical man. The grim reality of the Arab and Islamic world, and indeed of the world in general, make many a dream a practical goal to be realized in the interests of progress, harmony and peace. But what of Qadhdhafi's goal? It is best summed up in a letter which he sent in

1974 to the magazine *al-Usbu' al-'Arabi* in answer to a question which Sadat asked in an interview with the same magazine: 'What does Colonel Qadhdhafi want?'

What I wish is the following:

(1) Arab unity, with the merger of Egypt and Libya under the leadership of Sadat himself, as the nucleus of that unity.

(2) The liberation of Palestine, and the return of the Palestinian people to their homes, out of which they were forcibly evicted. This does not mean simply 'recognition of Palestinian rights' – this imperialistic expression which means nothing.

(3) The creation of an Arab industrial nuclear power, through Arab unity, ranking third in the world.

(4) The creation of an Islamic unity in which a united Arab nation would constitute an important part – even its center. This in order that it may give support to Muslims throughout the world to protect their lands and holy places and to demand due respect of this callous world. I wish the revival of Islam anew as a Divine ideology intended for all mankind.

(5) I wish for peace, brotherhood and equality among all human beings, and that we all arrive 'at a world of common accord'.[51]

Notes

1 *al-Kitab al-Akhdar*, part 3, pp. 117, 123.
2 Quoted in Marius K. Deeb, 'Islam and Arab Nationalism in Al-Qaddafi's Ideology', *Journal of South Asian and Middle Eastern Studies*, vol. 2, no. 2 (winter 1978), 12.
3 Muhammad Rashid Rida, *Tarikh al-Ustadh al-Imam Muhammad 'Abduh*, 3 vols. (Cairo, Matba'at al-Manar, 1350/1931), vol. 2, p. 506.
4 See *ibid.*, vol. 1, pp. 917–18; and see also Muhammad 'Abduh, *al-Islam wa-al-Nasraniyah ma'a al-'Ilm wa-al-Madaniyah* (a collection of articles originally published in the periodical *al-Manar*), 8th edn. (Cairo, Dar al-Manar, 1373/1954).
5 See 'Dhikra Salah al-Din wa-Ma'rakat Hittin', in *al-Manar*, vol. 8, no. 92, pp. 599–605.
6 The title of two of Arslan's major works: *Hadir al-'Alam al-Islami* and

Limadha ta'akhkhara al-Muslimun ('The Present Condition of the Muslim World' and 'Why Have the Muslims Fallen Behind?) best express his concerns.

7 See Ernest Dawn, *From Arabism to Ottomanism* (Chicago, University of Illinois Press, 1973), pp. 142–3.

8 *al-Sijill al-Qawmi*, vol. 14 (1982–83), p. 20.

9 *Ibid.*, p. 23.

10 *Ibid.*, vol. 5 (1973–74), pp. 156–61.

11 Qur'an 3:19.

12 *al-Sijill al-Qawmi*, vol. 6 (1974–75), p. 223.

13 *Ibid.*, vol. 5, pp. 321–32; see also pp. 318–22.

14 *Ibid.*, vol. 6, p. 263.

15 *Ibid.*, p. 264.

16 *Ibid.*, p. 293.

17 *Ibid.*, vol. 4, pp. 321–3.

18 Qur'an 9:6.

19 *al-Sijill al-Qawmi*, vol. 4, p. 324.

20 *Ibid.*, pp. 3–7.

21 *Ibid.*, p. 534.

22 *Ibid.*, p. 335.

23 This pamphlet is entitled '*Judhur al-Quwwah*' ('The roots of power'). It has no author, publisher or place or date of publication. It is, however, clearly a government-prepared and distributed document.

24 *Judhur al-Quwwah*, p. 28.

25 According to tradition, the Prophet was born on the Day of the Elephant – that is, when Abraha the Ethiopian general besieged the Ka'bah and had subsequently to withdraw because of Divine intervention. See Qur'an 105.

26 *Judhur al-Quwwah*, 29–30.

27 See, for example, Qur'an 26:195, 12:2 and 39:28.

28 See, for example, Qur'an 8:53, 9:56, 17:26 and 4:1.

29 See, for example, Qur'an 5:48 and 30:22.

30 *al-Sijill al-Qawmi*, vol. 3, p. 189.

31 *Ibid.*, pp. 310–312.

32 *Ibid.*, vol. 4, p. 32.

33 Qur'an 3:110.

34 *al-Sijill al-Qawmi*, vol. 4, p. 33.

35 Qur'an 3:103; *al-Sijill al-Qawmi*, vol 4, pp. 18–19.

36 Qur'an 2:143.

37 M. Ayoub, *The Qur'an and its Interpreters* (Albany, N.Y., SUNY Press, 1984), pp. 171–3.

38 *al-Sijill al-Qawmi*, vol. 4, p. 33.

39 *Ibid.*, vol. 10, p. 514.

40 Qur'an 3:64.

41 Qur'an 21:107 and 34:28.

42 *al-Sijill al-Qawmi*, vol. 6, p. 143.

43 Hasan Khalil Husayn, *al-Qadhdhafi wa-al-Thawrah al-Islamiyah* (Benghazi, Maktabat al-Andalus, 1973), p. 41.

44 See above, Chapter 2, p. 60 and *al-Kitab al-Akhdar*, part 3, pp. 173–4.

45 *al-Sijill al-Qawmi*, vol. 14, p. 893.

46 *Ibid.*, pp. 894–5.

47 *al-Nadwah al-'Alamiyah hawl Fikar Mu'mmar al-Qadhdhafi – al-Kitab al-Akhdar* (Free University of Madrid, 1–4 December 1980), part 1 (Paris, People's Bureau of the Libyan Popular Government, n.d.), p. 309.

48 *Ibid.*, pp. 310–11.

49 *Ibid.*, p. 311.

50 *Ibid.*, p. 311.

51 *al-Sijill al-Qawmi*, vol. 6, pp. 122–3. The phrase 'a word of common accord' is taken from the Qur'an: 3:63.

5
Qadhdhafi's Image

It should be evident from our discussion thus far that religion in general, and Islam in particular, plays a fundamental role in Mu'ammar al-Qadhdhafi's thought. His faith in, and commitment to, Islam have provided the primary focus, framework and impetus for his social ideas and political actions. They have also provided the basis of his image in both the Arab and Islamic world and the West. However, before we take a brief look at this image, it may be useful to take a closer look at Qadhdhafi's desert and Islamic roots.

Qadhdhafi's Roots

Because the desert, as we observed in the first chapter of this work, knows no walls and restrictions, the virtues and vices of its Bedouin inhabitants grow out of this freedom, a freedom often bordering on anarchy. What distinguished desert from town dwellers in ancient Arab society was not so much their nomadic life as the freedom which it expressed. The people of the desert had no kings, chiefs or notables. They knew no social hierarchy, as was common to the civilized societies surrounding them. A tribal chief was only 'a first among equals'. He presided over a small council of elders who ruled by persuasion rather than force or even the delegation of authority. The elders of a tribe played the role of wise men, preserved the tribe's honour and integrity and embodied its virtues of hospitality, bravery, and the cohesion of its internal as well as intertribal pacts and relations.

Pre-Islamic Arabs were not bound by the annals and records of history; rather, they told their tales in spontaneous outbursts of poetry. It was in poetry and cryptic aphorisms and proverbs that their philosophy, history and laws were enshrined. In short, the desert society to which Qadhdhafi is heir was a radically free and natural society governed by time-honoured traditions, social customs and religious beliefs and principles.[1]

Islam was born on the edge of the desert, and in a society based in desert life and traditions. It is this life and its traditions which gave Islam, as a religious and socio-political system, its essential framework. Islam came not to abolish these customs and traditions, but to reform and transform them into moral imperatives with an overarching religious purpose. Manly virtue [*muruwwah*], for example, was not denied, but transformed into moral and physical courage to be used not for show, but in defence of the weak, the orphan and the needy. It was transformed into a religious virtue.[2] Likewise, hospitality, which for pre-Islamic Arabs was mainly a show for poets to praise and for rivals to admire and envy, was transformed into the injunction to do good works 'in God's way'. Freedom, which meant in the time of *jahiliyah* each for himself, was transformed by Islam into the principle of *shura*, or consultation in all things on the basis of personal righteousness and veracity rather than power, wealth, or social prestige.[3]

These virtues continued to be reflected in the life of the first Muslim community after being reformed and reintegrated into a new faith, a new way of life and a new world-view. The Prophet himself adhered to the 'good' social customs of his society, yet, in keeping with his prophetic mission, he gave Arab and Muslim life a profoundly religious and moral orientation. He encouraged personal initiative, and consulted with his companions in all the affairs of the nascent state – in social affairs as well as the strategies of war.[4] The most crucial and enduring change which Islam brought into Arab society was a new source of Divine guidance – the Qur'an – which remains the final arbiter in all areas of the life of Muslim society. The Prophet's special authority rested on his prophetic prerogative. Yet this special prerogative was derived from the Qur'an to whose authority he, no less than any other Muslim, was subject.

The Qur'anic principle of *shura* operated in such an exemplary manner in the community of the first generation of Muslims that this period has remained normative for all subsequent generations. The ideal for the equality of all believers, inherent in the principle of *shura*, was staunchly defended by the *khawarij* ('seceders'), those who rebelled against the principle of authority based on nobility of lineage, worldly power or wealth rather than faith and righteousness. They seceded not only from 'Ali's camp, but from society altogether. They were the first revolutionaries of Islam[5] to advocate a sort of modern democracy, a kind of democracy in fact closely akin to the socio-political ideas of Qadhdhafi. Qadhdhafi has acknowledged this kinship in agreeing with the *Khawarij* that Muhammad was a prophet and not a king, and that he did not therefore appoint a successor.[6]

Muslim historians and traditionalists have regarded the age of the first four 'rightly-guided' caliphs as the only age of true caliphal succession. Henceforth, it is generally agreed, the caliphate became a kingship modelled on the imperial autocracies of Byzantium and Persia. 'Umar ibn al-Khattab, the second caliph, distinguished himself in the eyes of Byzantine and Persian aristocracy by being in no way distinguishable from any other Muslim of Madinah. The main fault of 'Uthman, the third caliph, according to early Muslim historians, was that he set up his relatives in authority 'over the necks of the people'. Indeed, it was social inequality and the illegitimate usurpation of the wealth of society by the few men of power which was behind all the revolts of early Islam. To a great extent it was the attempts of ruthless generals, kings and sultans to deprive Arab Muslim society of that freedom and dignity of the desert which shook the *ummah* of Islam to its foundations so soon after its establishment, and for many centuries to come.

The same socio-political and economic principles which governed early Muslim society and which produced such early revolutionary men who spoke out against poverty and oppression as 'Ali ibn Abi Talib and Abu Dharr al-Ghifari have not ceased to inspire Muslims in our time. A 'revolutionary' concept of Islam, such as the one Qadhdhafi espouses, is not new; it may even be said to be traditional throughout Islamic history. This is in some contrast to the Christian experience. 'Ali's opposition to poverty and inequality in society made him declare: 'Were poverty a man, I would have killed him with my sword!' A more concrete form of protest was 'Ali's own personal life of austerity and harsh discipline. Abu Dharr actually advocated revolution against the rich of society when he said, 'I marvel at a poor man – why he does not go out into the streets raising his sword against the people!' Abu Dharr had to pay dearly for his ideas: he died in exile.

As the revolutionaries of early Islam were feared and persecuted by the rich and powerful rulers, so are the revolutionaries of today. Qadhdhafi states that he wishes to follow the example of the Prophet who fought with such determination against oppression and inequality in society that Bilal the black slave became equal with his master Umayyah. He sees his own mission and the task of the Libyan revolution as having the same motivations and goal for modern Muslim society. The basic aim of *The Green Book* is to present in general and contemporary terms the ideals of justice and equality which Qadhdhafi sees in the Qur'an and the life of the Prophet and his community. The background of *The Green Book* is the life of the Prophet and his community. The background of *The Green Book* is the life of the desert, which has retained an amazing continuity from early Islam to the twentieth century. Like many of the Prophet's companions, Qadhdhafi is uncompromising in his views of right and wrong, as well as of the necessary measures to right the wrongs of society. They strove to change their society from the *jahiliyah* of idolatry and disregard for the rights of the weak and destitute to a society of total submission (*islam*) to God and concern for the welfare of his creatures. In like manner, Qadhdhafi looks to the same kind of simple, dedicated and uncompromising society to do battle against the *jahiliyah* of today's ideological idolatry, materialism and economic and political oppression.

The primary source of inspiration for Qadhdhafi's Third Universal Theory is the Islamic ideal of equality and justice on which the Islamic polity was founded. The idea of direct democracy, or rule of the masses without any mediation, is the basis of a system in which Divine law (*shari'ah*) and social customs (*'urf*) are harmoniously amalgamated. The notion harks back to the Prophet's society where Arab custom was remoulded by Qur'anic morality. The belief that all authority in the end belongs to God – 'God is most great' – makes any human temporal authority relative and ephemeral. This in turn leads to the rejection of absolute power as embodied in traditional systems of hierarchical authority. Finally, this also leads to the rejection of any source of power which does not have Divine sanction. This sanction is seen by Qadhdhafi in the Qur'anic charge to humanity to be 'God's representative on earth'.[7] Humanity is for Qadhdhafi not an abstract principle, but the masses. Hence, collective authority, or 'direct rule of the masses', is a sacred trust; it is God's rule through his human representatives.

The fundamental principle on which Islamic political ideology rests is God's absolute sovereignty: His sole prerogative to rule, to command and to forbid. Likewise, Islamic economic ideology rests on the principle of God's absolute dominion over His creation. On the basis of this principle, Qadhdhafi constructed an economic theory which presupposes God's lordship over all wealth and man's stewardship only. Thus man is responsible finally to God and to society for the manner in which he discharges his responsibilities over God's wealth. In the principle of *zakat* as well as in all aspects of social responsibility, it is God who has legislated the laws which govern the just distribution and consumption of God's wealth. Again, these ideals are dramatically presented in the Qur'an: 'To God belongs the inheritance of the heavens and the earth', and 'We [God] shall inherit the earth and all that is in it'.[8]

The basic Islamic principles we have been discussing are in themselves accepted by all Muslims. It is not Islam as traditionally understood and practised which is the basis of Mu'ammar al-Qadhdhafi's quarrel with the Arab religious and political establishment, but rather his uncompromising faith in the truth as he sees it. This too is one of the characteristics of early Muslim society, as well as of the desert society of which Qadhdhafi is a product. The Prophet's Makkan compatriots objected to Islam because it was something novel, and thus a threat to their life style and the 'established tradition' (*sunnah*) of their ancestors.[9] Yet the Muslims persisted: they fought battles and used persuasion until finally Islam itself became the *sunnah* of Arab society and countless other millions of men and women throughout the world. As an established order, however, Islam was protected from change, even positive change. The following alleged *hadith* of the Prophet, repeated still in many Friday prayer sermons, has forever closed the door of change: 'Every novelty [*muhdathah*] is a [reprehensible] innovation [*bid'ah*]; every innovation is an error [*dalalah*], and every error shall lead to the Fire.' Qadhdhafi is, in the eyes of many Muslims of the establishment, an innovator.

In October 1979, Colonel Qadhdhafi addressed an international symposium on *The Green Book*, held at Qar Yunus in Benghazi. He asserted that *The Green Book*, as a guide to a new social order, would inevitably prevail. This inevitability was due to the fact that all previous revolutions and struggles for the attainment of a 'better society' had resulted in failure. It was inevitable, therefore, that a 'new society of the masses' would be established world-wide. It was possible, Qadhdhafi argued further, that temporary setbacks might occur, and social chaos and dictatorship might again prevail. But these would only be passing episodes in the march of history towards this noble goal. This eagerly awaited new society would, in accordance with the principles of *The Green Book*, be free from all political, social and economic conflicts. In the new society all traditional and repressive laws and traditions would forever vanish. But for all this to come into effect, 'All the methodologies which are followed now in the world must be destroyed by an international intellectual revolution which would liberate humankind from all fanatical systems which have intentionally aimed at remolding the taste, conceptual and rational faculties of human beings.'[10]

Qadhdhafi's confidence in this social ideal is based on the conviction that this philosophy represents the only true realization of the social values of the Qur'an. On 1 February 1983, the leader assured the participants in the General People's Congress that the Libyan miracle of the achievement of popular authority is a historical inevitability for all human society. But this had been possible in Libya because only there, and 'for the first time since the time of the Messenger, the Qur'an is being applied'. Colonel Qadhdhafi then declared: 'You shall see the true Qur'an. You shall know that all that is now done in the Muslim world (in the name of the Qur'an) is not of the Qur'an; it is pretense! These are only laws promulgated by people with certain vested interests: interests in polygamy and slave trade, the interests of those who have reserves of gold, and own big businesses. It is this corrupt class which promulgated such false laws in the name of Islam.'[11]

It is clear then that Qadhdhafi sees himself as a leader of a revolution with a special mission: the task of reforming and uniting the Arab nation, and under its leadership, the Third World. In a national Arab opposition convention, held on 17 February 1983, he pledged unconditional assistance and support to any secret revolutionary movement which might arise in the Arab world. He then angrily berated Arab rulers: 'Is this Islam? Who gives support to the American arsenal? It is Arab oil! Islamic oil! Is this Islam? Islam exists only in the Qur'an.' Qadhdhafi cited again the Qur'anic reproach of those who hoard gold and silver and do not spend it in God's cause (Qur'an 9:34). He then asked: 'Where is the bond of right [*halal*] and wrong [*haram*]? Is this Islam?[12]

Qadhdhafi's Image in the Arab World

Colonel Qadhdhafi's relationship with other Arab heads of state is one of conflict and confrontation. From Qadhdhafi's point of view, it is a confrontation between right and wrong, progress and reaction. From the viewpoint of his detractors, it is a confrontation between atheism and faith, between Islam and non-Islam.

In the interest of Arab and Muslim unity, however, Qadhdhafi is ready to cooperate with Arab rulers with whom he has little in common apart from their Arab and Islamic identity. The union between Libya, a popularly ruled country, and the kingdom of Morocco is a clear illustration of his point. Still, Qadhdhafi's image among his own Arab brothers is one of enigmatic or at best ambivalent character. They cannot ignore, or even disagree with his nationalist fervour and the bitter truths of defeat and humiliation which the Arab nation has suffered in Palestine and the Lebanon, truths of which Qadhdhafi is constantly reminding them.

To a large extent, the image of Mu'ammar al-Qadhdhafi which the official media of some Arab countries have portrayed is based on hostile information propagated by Western, and particularly American, media sources. The image which these sources have fostered is intended for public consumption. Only by discrediting Qadhdhafi's integrity of faith can his opponents hope to convince the Arab masses of their anti-Qadhdhafi propaganda. Qadhdhafi's negative image is often used to divert public attention in the Arab world from foreign policies of certain Arab governments, which are generally seen as deleterious to Arab interests, such as the Camp David agreement and domestic problems of corruption, negligence and blatant repression.

We have already observed Qadhdhafi's view of the *hajj* pilgrimage as an international annual Islamic event, and his call for freeing this important religious rite from the control of any particular state authority. In a controversial sermon which he delivered in October 1980, on the occasion of the Islamic feast of sacrifice, Qadhdhafi called in strong and unequivocal terms for the liberation of the skies of the holy cities of Makkah and Madinah from American domination. At the same time that he issued this general call, Colonel Qadhdhafi sent a strongly worded message to the Saudi king and the rulers of the Gulf states. The tone and language of both sermon and telegraphic message, and the response they evoked, are important for a clearer understanding of Qadhdhafi's priorities, as well as his public image.

Qadhdhafi began by reminding his fellow worshippers that the spot where they were praying contained the remains of great martyrs among the Prophet's companions, martyrs who conquered these lands and built the first Islamic capital in this desert. They struggled in the way of God: 'they are not dead, rather they are alive with their Lord sustained'.[13] 'Whoever wants to follow in their footsteps', Qadhdhafi continued, 'whoever wishes to remain alive and never die, let him endeavor to be martyred in the way of God.'[14]

Qadhdhafi then informed his audience that as they were then celebrating the feast of sacrifice, the Ka'bah was under the yoke of American occupation. The day before, he observed, the sounds of the pilgrims on Mount 'Arafat were intermingled with the din of American aeroplanes. The pilgrimage has thus lost all meaning. It has reverted to its pre-Islamic character as in the time of *jahiliyah*. Colonel Qadhdhafi went on:

> Unfortunately, some Christians, leaders of the new crusade, have succeeded in occupying Makkah, the Radiant City [Madinah] and the Mount of 'Arafat with their airplanes. Their AWACs yesterday caused an interruption in the broadcast over the radio stations throughout the Muslim world, which were carrying the events of the standing on the sacred Mount of 'Arafat. This was caused by interference in the air waves by the American airplanes which have been flying over Makkah, over the tomb of the Messenger and over Mount 'Arafat.'[15]

Qadhdhafi then asked: 'What meaning does the *hajj* have this year and in years to come as well, so long as American occupation of the Sacred House of God continues? The only meaning left for us is fighting, it is the struggle [*jihad*] for the liberation of the House of God.' He then called on all Muslims everywhere to put away their prayer beads, and their copies of the Qur'an if necessary, and to take up arms instead, in this difficult hour. He called on them to shun wealth and prestige, to resist exploitation and deception and to seek death in the way of God. He then declared: 'To be engaged in the battle of *jihad* today is better than the worship of a thousand years with egotistical litanies of praise and penitent devotion. Islam is the religion of power, of challenge, of steadfastness and of *jihad*.

It behoves us, therefore, to scatter our prayer beads, if they were to keep our hands away from arms. We should put our copies of the Qur'an on the shelf if they were to distract us from implementing its teachings', Qadhdhafi insisted.[16]

In the telegram sent to the Saudi monarch and other Gulf heads of state, Colonel Qadhdhafi expressed his disquiet at the steady American military penetration of the Arab peninsula and the Gulf, the potential conflicts this could create, as well as the hollow claims and justifications accompanying it. These claims and justifications, Qadhdhafi added, signify no more than America's designs to colonize Arab lands. This penetration has been consciously planned and executed with the help of the Zionist state, and is rapidly spreading through the Gulf, and into Egypt and Palestine. The final aim of this increasing military presence is for America and the Zionists to deprive the Arab world of its independence. Qadhdhafi then cautioned: 'If Arab [rulers] were to agree on ending their independence in return for remaining kings and presidents, then this American military penetration, which is sure to destroy our very existence, will be completed peacefully and without any resistance.' Qadhdhafi concluded: 'Thus in our estimation this action, which in no way can be considered as a pact of friendship or alliance, is no more than our acceptance of the loss of our independence.'[17]

Qadhdhafi then argued that such reasons for America's increasing military presence as the problem of Afghanistan, the Iran–Iraq war, or the issue of the security of energy sources and the price of oil are all merely excuses. Arabs, therefore, should not let themselves fall victim to the conflicts between the two super powers. America, he observed, has justified its presence in Arab lands by the Soviet invasion of Afghanistan. But if America was really interested in Afghanistan, then its armies should be sent to fight there. Moreover, America had used the Iran–Iraq conflict to justify sending its advanced warning aeroplanes into the Arab peninsula, and had been urging the Gulf states to enter with it into long-term defensive alliances.[18]

Colonel Qadhdhafi is not simply a political theorist; he is a committed leader for a revolution. He is, therefore, compelled by his own religious and ideological commitment to support, and even participate in, any organized resistance to the schemes of the super powers against Arab independence and self-determination. He thus advised the King and his fellow shaykhs and princes of his intention to resist their pro-American policies. He said: 'Let it be known that

we shall resist America in the Arab homeland!' Qadhdhafi distinguishes between the Christians of the Crusades in the modern
colonial forms from the Christians whom the Qur'an describes as
'nearest in amity to the people of faith'.[19] He describes the conflict
between the Muslims today with Western powers in terms of the
Crusades of the Middle Ages, which have unfortunately cast their
shadow over the history of all subsequent Muslim–Christian relations. He writes: 'This confrontation is only another stage in the
continuing cycle of Crusader wars between Islam and Christianity,
between the East and West, and between the Muslim *ummah* and
the Frankish nation. Thus it is our Islamic duty to ally ourselves with
the Muslims of Iran in this confrontation with the ongoing crusade,
instead of waging war against them on behalf of America.'[20]

We have analyzed these two texts at some length because they
typify well Qadhdhafi's revolutionary attitude towards Arab unity
and Western threats to it. It must also be added that Qadhdhafi
speaks for many Arabs who are frustrated with the present political,
social and economic conditions of their potentially affluent and
strong nation. It is no surprise, therefore, that Qadhdhafi's remarks
evoked a strong reaction in the Arab religious and political establishment. It is beyond the scope and purpose of this work to
analyze Arab media coverage of this response. We shall content
ourselves with presenting the objections and accusations published
in the official journal of the Muslim World League, a religious organ
of the Saudi establishment.[21]

Among the many accusations levelled against Mu'ammar al-
Qadhdhafi were the following. He was accused of being a spearhead
against Islam, because he is intent on the distintegration of Muslim
unity. He was also accused of imprisoning pilgrims on their return
from the *hajj* only because they may disapprove his straying from
the fold of Islam. Qadhdhafi's ultimate aim is, the journal stated, to
abolish the pilgrimage.

Qadhdhafi's view of education is an integral part of his theory of
the 'free new society' as presented in the third part of *The Green
Book*. The form and extent of the education of any member of this
society must be freely determined by him or her. It must also be
freely offered outside the framework of traditional classroom
education. On the basis of this idea, the Muslim World League
accused him of demanding the abolition of education.

Because his ideas are considered to be totally misleading, the
journal suggested that Qadhdhafi be excluded from all fields of

international Islamic endeavour. It even suggested that he had signed a defence treaty with the Soviet Union, which in fact he has never done. Qadhdhafi was further accused of spreading doubt among the Muslims in the prophetic *sunnah*. Thus he was accused of having arrested all Libyan *ulama'* who had opposed him, and leaving them to languish in prison.

Qadhdhafi's opposition to polygamy was considered as an act of *kufr*, or rejection of faith. Likewise, his alleged opposition to the veil was considered as a calumny against the Qur'an. In spite of Qadhdhafi's antipathy to communism and Zionism, he was accused of preventing the Muslims from resisting them both.

The Muslim World League's journal decreed Mu'ammar al-Qadhdhafi's rejection of faith on the basis of eight specific accusations: his alleged denial of the authority of the *sunnah*; his alleged doubts in the soundness of certain Qur'anic texts; his alleged claim of prophethood; his denial of the Qur'an's sanctions of polygamy; his denial of the Qur'anic prescription of the veil for women; his abolition of the traditional *hijrah* calendar; his alleged call for the abolition of the obligation of pilgrimage; and, finally, his support of the Russian occupation of Afghanistan.[22]

As we have already dealt with most of these points, it is not necessary to discuss them again here. It is, however, important to observe that Qadhdhafi has never doubted the Qur'an or questioned its authority. Nor has he denied the authority of the Prophet's *sunnah*. His doubt of certain *hadith* traditions has been shared by many *hadith* scholars throughout Muslim history. He does not reject *hadith* in principle, but only those whose soundness or authenticity cannot be ascertained. His aversion to polygamy as a means simply of satisfying man's lust has also been widely shared by Muslim thinkers. He has been calling not for the abolition of the *hajj*, but for its purification and the restoration of its meaning and significance for today's Muslim community. His view of the importance of the *hijrah* of the Prophet, and hence its use as the basis of the Islamic calendar, may be open to question. But neither this view, nor any of the other accusations levelled against him constitute a basis for the charge of infidelity. Finally, he has constantly demonstrated his opposition to the Russian occupation of Afghanistan, and his active support to the Afghan *mujahidin*.

Qadhdhafi's ideas and actions present a direct threat to the power and position of all Arab rulers. Their criticisms and condemnations of his ideas are part of the image which they have attempted to project of a man who stands diametrically opposed to the entire system of Arab political, social, economic and religious traditional values. Many of the educated Arab youth, therefore, listen to Qadhdhafi's speeches and declarations on the Libyan radio, 'The Voice of the Great Arab Nation', with intense interest. They find in them an expression of both their hopes and frustrations, but above all of their shared dream of Arab unity.

Qadhdhafi is considered as a danger not only to Arab stability, but also to the interests of the West and the communist world in this so-called stability. The image of Qadhdhafi in the West may differ in form and content from that projected by the Arab establishment. In their purpose, however, they are one. We shall conclude this study with a brief glance at Qadhdhafi's image in the West.

Qadhdhafi's Image in the West

In the West, Qadhdhafi has become a myth of many dimensions. He is at one and the same time the desert 'horseman of God' and the 'messenger of the desert'[23] as well as the conceited fascist and great international menace.

On 3 November 1985, the *Washington Post* carried on its front page the following headline: 'CIA Anti-Qadhdhafi Plan Backed, Reagan Authorizes Covert Operation to Undermine Libyan Regime.' This American plan and the reasons for its authorization tell the fantastic tale of Qadhdhafi's image in America. The plan calls for the support of countries in North Africa which may be persuaded to destabilize the Libyan regime. Alternatively, it calls for some sort of covert operation which would first 'disrupt, pre-empt and frustrate Qaddafi's subversive and terrorist plans'. Secondly, the plan was to lure Qadhdhafi into some adventure, or 'terrorist exploit' which would encourage the Libyan military to seize power. Such misadventure was then to provide an ostensible justification for either Algeria or Egypt to invade Libya and over-throw Qadhdhafi.

This plan, which was intentionally or unintentionally leaked to the press, has been in the making for some years – that is, since not long after the beginning of Ronald Reagan's presidency. Since 1981, the American Central Intelligence Agency has been giving financial support to groups of Libyan dissidents in exile, but to no avail. This is because, a well-informed intelligence/officer said, they are 'only boy scouts'. It is generally agreed that in fact there is no well-organized and effective movement against the Libyan regime inside or outside the country. Qadhdhafi still enjoys popularity as the 'leader of the revolution' in spite of alleged domestic problems and mounting foreign pressures. This is the main reason why America has not been successful in overthrowing Qadhdhafi.

The main reason given by the Reagan administration for this plan is that Qadhdhafi is a 'menace to U.S. interests'. The 'plan', we are told, was intended to stop terrorism, and not to support attempts to assassinate the Libyan leader.

It is important to note that opposition to the 'anti-Qadhdhafi plan' came from officials in the U.S. government who are opposed to American involvement in international assassination plots. However, a top secret 'Vulnerability Assessment' document prepared by the C.I.A. and other intelligence agencies, dated 18 June 1984, concluded that, 'no course of action short of stimulating Qadhdhafi's fall could bring any significant and enduring change in Libyan policy'. The report recommended that disaffected elements in the Libyan military be either encouraged to attempt to assassinate Qadhdhafi, or at least to cooperate with exiles working against the Libyan regime. The 'secret document' further recommended 'a broad program in cooperation with key countries, combining political, economic and paramilitary actions'. This would also have included acts of sabotage by groups of exiles backed by the United States. The report notes that Egypt, Iraq, Sudan and Tunisia have been assisting dissident groups operating in exile.

There is no doubt that this entire plan is, by all international standards, a classic case of state terrorism. There must be compelling reasons for a government like that of the United States even to contemplate such a plan against a sovereign state. The primary justification for this action – that Qadhdhafi is internationally a menace to U.S. interests – has already been noted. More specifically, however, Qadhdhafi is reportedly supporting some thirty insurgent, radical or terrorist groups in various parts of the world. The countries named are noteworthy. They include Nicaragua and El Salvador, Pakistan, the Philippines, the Lebanon, and several other countries in Africa, Europe and Latin America. Another, and equally important reason, is the alleged presence of thousands of East European advisers in Libya today.

The liberation movements in many of these countries stand in sharp contrast to the repressive governments which depend on U.S. support for their existence. Furthermore, these so-called terrorist movements enjoy wide international sympathy. The international community would do well to examine the relationship of the violence committed by liberation movements and state violence: torture, oppression and the flagrant violation of human rights to life and liberty, by many repressive regimes. It must then be honestly and candidly decided what in reality constitutes terrorism.

Many Western academics, journalists and United Nations observers have noted, sometimes reluctantly, the phenomenal transformation of Libya since the revolution. One of the most striking aspects of this change has been the display of national pride, self-confidence and dignity on all levels of Libyan society. The well-known American journalist John Cooley reports, with typical Western condescending arrogance, that he greatly offended his official guide when he suggested that he bribe the customs official to let him jump the line. The young official's retort is instructive: 'We don't have this kind of thing here. . . . We stopped that long ago.'[24] Mr Cooley evinces the interesting approach of so many Westerners interested in anything Arab, Middle Eastern or Islamic. It is to scorn and deride, and if the Arab or Muslim country or individual happens to be an ally, to treat the whole thing as quaint oriental exotica. Orientals cannot think for themselves, so whenever they write or say something important, some Western source must be found from which such a person must have derived his ideas. Qadhdhafi's ideas then are based on Arabic translations of a 'mixed bag of philosophy, sociology, history and pseudo-history'. This wide but random reading of Western sources includes, Cooley believes, 'fascist theory as applied in the corporate states of Mussolini in Italy, and De Oliveira Salazar in Portugal'.[25] The fascist element in Qadhdhafi's thought appears, according to Cooley, in his emphasis on blood relations as a prime factor in the formation of a tribe, and consequently of a nation. Although all three parts of *The Green Book* unmistakably present the same style and idiom in Arabic, Cooley, who himself does not appear to know Arabic, accepts the allegation that the third part of *The Green Book* is the work of a ghost writer who may have been a student of Hegel, or possibly Marx.

The influence of 'fascist theory' can hardly be seen in a simple attention to tribal solidarity. Such a preoccupation springs naturally from Qadhdhafi's own Bedouin background and the organically tribal nature of the society of which he is a part. It may be that Mr Cooley means by this remark deliberately to offend. He cannot be entirely ignorant of modern Libyan history, of the long and bloody struggle of the Libyans against Italian occupation and colonization, and particularly of the sufferings and heroic resistance of the Libyan people and its scattered and underequipped Bedouin forces against Italian Fascist forces, and against Fascist-inspired Italian settlement for the purpose of *Lebensraum* on their vital agricultural lands.[26] Italian Fascism is a bitter and ever-present memory for Libyans, the culminating stage in a long history of Italian encroachment and atrocities. The final expulsion of the last Italian '*pied-noirs*', after the *al-fatih* revolution, is seen by Libyans, Qadhdhafi included, as the final defeat of Italian Fascism; as Qadhdhafi himself says, 'This heroic people knows well the nature of Italian imperialism, and remembers in particular that it sacrificed half of its population for the liberation of its country.'[27]

Qadhdhafi is known to be an avid reader on all kinds of subjects. That *The Green Book* bears some similarities to Western thought is not the point at issue. Rather, the fact is that any cursory reading of *The Green Book* reveals its basic source and background. It is essentially the result of Qadhdhafi's Islamic background and up-bringing, his social milieu and the struggles and aspirations of his people. Although it is not an Islamic work, none the less it is born out of the Islamic spirit of reform and concern for the well-being of society.

Cooley's otherwise informative book on Libya suffers from a derisive tongue in cheek, and hence highly subjective approach. It represents one kind of a hostile image typical of the American press and other communication media. A more ideologically motivated hostile image is that presented by the leftist South African journalist Ruth First. Her main objection to the Libyan revolution is that it is Islamic in character. It is an unreal or 'elusive' revolution. She writes: 'At first sight as at last, there is no revolution more contradictory and perverse than the Libyan.' This is because, in the view of Ms First, 'It claims to be a social revolution that would bring Libya into the company of the great twentieth century revolutions of social liberation, yet it zealously pursues a revival of Islamic fundamentalism.' Libya's fault is, then, according to Ruth First, that it is at one and the same time an Islamic and a revolutionary state. Of course, the two can never go together. Ruth First's list of seeming contradictions in the Libyan revolution reflects more her own hostility to Islam rather than an objective assessment of a revolution which, like all other revolutions, has its mistakes and ideals. She wonders how anyone could see in the starry-eyed simplistic and ruthless man, which she takes Qadhdhafi to be, even the faintest possibility for bringing about reform in the Arab world. She asks: 'Is it to be a case of pristine Bedouin morality steeped in the fundamentalist morality of the seventh century, riding in from the desert to reform twentieth century state craft? Is this possible in our day and age?'[28]

Ruth First shares the Western misconception that Islam is simply a seventh-century phenomenon totally alien to the life of modern society. The truth is, however, that Islam has endured for over fourteen hundred years as a source of moral and spiritual strength in the lives of millions of people, largely outside the desert of Arabia. Modern history has, moveover, demonstrated that borrowed ideas and ideals do not make a revolution. Change, if it is to be at all genuine, useful and long-term, must come out of the history and tradition of the people concerned. Thus, Islam, and Islam alone, will be capable of bringing reform not only to Libya, but to all the countries of the Muslim world.

In sharp contrast to Ms First's aversion to the desert, Mme Mirella Bianco was fascinated with the desert and its unique cultural and spiritual traditions. Her image of Qadhdhafi, while being positive and highly complimentary, is still somewhat distorted. Her view of Qadhdhafi as a sincere, spontaneous and genuine son of the desert is shared by many who knew him as intimately as she did. Yet it must be recognized that Qadhdhafi is a reformer, and not a prophet.

In the epilogue to her biography of Mu'ammar al-Qadhdhafi, Mme Bianco asks: 'O messenger of God, were you too a shepherd?' Qadhdhafi is made to reply: 'Yes, and there was no prophet who was not a shepherd!' It is on the basis of this literary device of a hypothetical question and answer that the Muslim World League journal accused Qadhdhafi of claiming to be a prophet. Be that as it may, Mme Bianco's apology for, and justification of, this comparison are instructive. She writes: 'I sincerely hope that the Libyan leader as well as my Muslim friends will believe my assurance that nothing would be more distasteful to me than to offend, even inadvertently, their religious feelings, or worse still, the veneration with which they surround the personage of the Prophet Muhammad.' She then argues that because Muhammad is held by

Muslims to be mortal, a reformer who has provided the model for all subsequent generations to emulate, that she made this comparison. The points which she sees in common between Qadhdhafi and the Prophet Muhammad are noteworthy. Both the Prophet and Qadhdhafi are Bedouins of a similar desert background. They both share, therefore, a common love for freedom, physical endurance, and an ideal of equality in society. They are both given to meditation, and share the belief that no real change in society could occur without a spiritual transformation. Both share a feeling of urgency in having to convey their vision of the universe to others. They are both teachers with unshakeable certainty in the rightness of their convictions. They both possess unusual courage, and an indomitable determination to pursue their mission. Finally, they are products of similar moments of transition and change in human history.[29]

The idea of comparing anyone with a personality like that of the Prophet Muhammad is dangerous, but only if by this is meant the elevation of such a person to the status of the prophet. Equally dangerous would be the possible conclusion that what Qadhdhafi, in this case, has said or done possesses the same authority as the Prophetic *sunnah*, or worse still, that of the Qur'an. Yet in a concrete way, all Muslims are enjoined to strive to emulate the Prophet's example by adopting his *sunnah* as their model of conduct. There is, to my knowledge, no evidence that Mu'ammar al-Qadhdhafi ever saw himself as more than what he is to his fellow Libyans, 'the brother colonel' or 'the brother leader'.

The sad point of Qadhdhafi's image in the West, and particularly in America, is that it is unfounded and counterproductive. In a letter which he sent to Carter and Reagan in October 1980, during their presidential campaigns, he expressed the wish that Libya and the United States could have developed a close and enduring friendship. He wrote: 'We would have liked to maintain friendship with America, especially since past relations between America and the Arab nation have not been marred by colonialism, as were our relations with certain European countries such as France, Britain and Italy, as they did colonize parts of our homeland.' He then observed that attempts to cement this friendship began at the time when the late Nasser came to power. But America lost that opportunity by taking inimical attitudes towards the Arab nation, thus losing a historic possibility of a productive friendship. Nasser was thus obliged to turn to the Soviet Union.

Qadhdhafi observed further that after the death of Nasser, Libya again tried to establish friendship with America, but again failed. This is because America treated this second attempt with the same inimical spirit, and thus another opportunity was lost. America undertook a number of provocative actions against Libya, including political, economic and propaganda measures which were exceedingly hostile. 'Thus', he concluded, 'America alone must bear the responsibility for the dangerous state which now exists. In fact America has left no room', Qadhdhafi noted, 'for any future attempts to establish friendship between the American and Arab nations.'

Qadhdhafi suggested that now the Arab and American nations should try to find a way to prevent armed conflict between the two countries. This could only be achieved if the United States withdraws all its forces from Arab lands, Arab waters and Arab skies.

Qadhdhafi then repeated many of the points which he made in the message to the Gulf rulers. He argued that it was America which had been violating Arab skies and waters, and thus it alone would be held responsible for any eventualities. The Arab peoples had the legitimate right to defend themselves, to use their oil wealth in their best interest, since it was their only means of income. He thus argued that if America gives itself the right to protect its interests in Arab oil, then the Arabs who are the owners of this commodity have the right to protect their own interests.

Colonel Qadhdhafi finally called for a radical change in America's policies of exploitation of other peoples. They must instead adopt a policy of equality among all nations regardless of their power, race or status. He concluded:

> We now see through these clarifications that America stands at a crossroads – either that it follows the path of peace by withdrawing its forces from the Arab homeland . . . that it leaves Arab oil for the Arabs, and that it stays neutral in the Middle East – or that it continues to follow the path of aggression and war. For the sake of peace and the prevention of world conflagration, and in order that we fulfill our human responsibility, we have sent this historic message to you. If you too love peace and are, like us anxious to save the world from disaster, I suggest that your election campaign be based on a new policy of peace for the United States, a policy based on the realities which we have

mentioned. Then you can convey this policy to all Americans – Arabs, Jews, Blacks and Amerindians – who would support you and give you their votes. We too would then support you and stand by you.[30]

Alas, American politics have not changed. The events in the Middle East during the Reagan presidency have all but destroyed any glimmer of hope for trust and friendship between the United States and the Arab world. Yet it cannot be denied that America remains a haven of refuge, even for many Arabs who are bitterly opposed to American policies in the Middle East. Libyans also wish for better relations and cooperation with America, but of course on the basis of equality and respect for the rights of human dignity of both peoples.

Behind Qadhdhafi's seemingly uncompromising ideological positions stands the hope for a better world. That he sees his vision of society as the road to the attainment of this hope is typical of every ideological reformer. It is also the ideal of Islam, as it is of every universal faith. Qadhdhafi's vision may be Utopian, but it is universal. That it is dogmatic in its assertiveness is a characteristic of the desert – the desert of men brave and free, of visionaries and prophets – 'We are on our way to transform the world into a *jamahiriya* [populist republic] not a Libyan *jamahiriya*, but a universal *jamahiriya*, as an end in itself. It is a *jamahiriya* which shall be an earthly paradise that may be realized. It is a *jamahiriya* which will be the 'lost paradise', the 'virtuous city' of which humanity dreams.'[31]

Mu'ammar al-Qadhdhafi's tireless struggle for Arab unity is based on the Qur'anic injunction for all Muslims to 'Hold fast all together to the rope of God and not be dispersed'.[32] The Arabs are the first guardians of the Islamic message because it is expressed in their language and cultural framework, and because it was they who first carried it to the rest of the world. Thus without Arab unity, the unity of the rest of the Muslim community would at best be a difficult undertaking.

Qadhdhafi's vision of a just society based on socialist principles is also grounded in the Islamic view of the basic equality of all human beings as created by God in the natural state (*fitrah*) of essential goodness: 'It is the *fitrah* of God, in which he created humankind; there can be no alteration of God's creation.'[33]

The ideal of social welfare and justice has led many in both the

Muslim and Christian communities to radical socialist movements. Qadhdhafi's ideas have much in common with the radical movements of liberation theology among the oppressed peasants and workers of Latin America. This is not a mere coincidence; rather, the conditions of extreme poverty and wealth, political frustration and national struggle, as well as the strategic importance of both Latin America and the Arab world for the United States and its multinational companies are contributory factors in the ideological and political affinities between Mu'ammar al-Qadhdhafi and the thinkers of Latin America. In fact, such radical socialist measures as Colonel Qadhdhafi has advocated are not unknown in Muslim history. The great revolt of the Zanj slaves working in the salt marshes of southern Iraq in the late ninth century is one of many examples of 'socialist' movements in the name of Islam against the oppression and injustice of the Muslim establishment. Indeed, it is this struggle against social evil which is the true meaning of *jihad* in Islam.

It is, finally, important to ask why Qadhdhafi supports so many revolutionary movements in so many parts of the world. This too can be justified on the basis of the Islamic injunction to help those who are oppressed, regardless of their creed, nationality or race. The Qur'an declares, 'We wish to bestow our favor on those who are oppressed in the earth to make them foremost among men, and to make them heirs.'[34] Mu'ammar al-Qadhdhafi and the Libyan people have for long struggled against all sorts of oppression. They therefore see it as their duty to help others in the same struggle. They too will continue to strive towards the attainment of the rich rewards which God, according to Islam, has promised those who help others in need.

Notes

1 The most authoritative study of pre-Islamic society is Jawad 'Ali, *al-Mufassal fi Tarikh al-'Arab qabl al-Islam*, 2nd edn., 10 vols. (Beirut, Dar al-'Ilm lil-Malayin, 1978), vol. 4, pp. 271ff.
2 Ignaz Goldziher, *Muslim Studies*, vol. 1 (London, George Allen and Unwin, 1967), pp. 11–44.
3 Qur'an 42:37–40.
4 A good example of this is the event of al-Khandaq (the Trench), during

which the Prophet accepted the novel suggestion of Salman the Persian to dig a trench around Madinah as a defensive measure.

5 'Umar Abu Nasr, *al-Khawarij fi al-Islam*, 3rd edn. (Beirut, Maktabat Abu Nasr, 1970) provides a good discussion of the Khawarij from the point of view of contemporary political thought.

6 *al-Sijill al-Qawmi*, vol. 4 (1972–73), p. 30.

7 Qur'an 2:30.

8 Qur'an 3:180 and 19:40. See also R. Garaudy, 'al-Islam wa-al-Shumuliyah fi al-'Amal al-Siyasi li-Mu'ammar al-Qadhdhafi' in *al-Nadwah al-'Alamiyah Hawl Fikr Mu'ammar al-Qadhdhafi – al-Kitab al-Akhdar* (Caracas, Central University, 1981), pp. 39–48.

9 Qur'an 5:104.

10 *al-Nadwah al-'Alamiyah Hawl al-Kitab al-Akhdar*, 2 vols. (Qar Yunus University, Benghazi, 1–3 Oct. 1979), vol. 1 (Paris, Markaz International, n.d.), p. 525; see also pp. 513ff.

11 *al-Sijill al-Qawmi*, vol. 14 (1982–83), p. 507.

12 *Ibid.*, vol. 14 (1982–83), pp. 395–6.

13 Qur'an 3:169.

14 Pamphlet, untitled (Ottawa: Manshurat al-Zahf al-Akhdar, 1981, 4th edn., containing a sermon delivered on the occasion of the Feast of Sacrifice, 1980), p. 8.

15 *Ibid.*, p. 8.

16 *Ibid.*, pp. 9–13.

17 *Ibid.*, pp. 17–18.

18 *Ibid.*, p. 18.

19 Qur'an 5:84.

20 Pamphlet, untitled (Ottawa: Manshurat al-Zahf al-Akhdar, 1981, 4th edn., containing a sermon delivered on the occasion of the Feast of Sacrifice, 1980), p. 19.

21 *Akhbar al-'Alam al-Islami* (Makkah Muslim World League), no. 694, 18 Dhu al-Hijjah 1401/27 Oct. 1980.

22 See Muhammad ibn 'Abd al-Karim al-Jaza'iri, *al-Qadhdhafi wa-al-Mutaqawwilun alayh* (Beirut, Dar 'Uqbah bin Nafi' lil-Nahr, 1982), pp. 11–15. The author deals with each accusation in detail, and attempts to show that such ideas do not constitute infidelity to Islam.

23 These epithets are even used as the titles of two books written on Qadhdhafi: *Kadhafi, le Templier d'Allah* (by Anne-Marie Cazalis) and *Kadhafi, Messager du desert* (by Mirella Bianco).

24 John Cooley, *Libyan Sandstorm* (New York, Holt, Rinehart and Winston, 1982), p. 130.

25 *Ibid.*, p. 144.

26 Claudio C. Segre, *Fourth Shore* (Chicago, University of Chicago Press, 1974), provides a detailed study of the motivations and methods of Italy throughout the colonial period, although it is not concerned with de-

tailing the effects of Italian policies on Libya.

27 *al-Sijill al-Qawmi*, vol. 4 (1972–73), p. 49. The history and folk history of Libyan resistance has unfortunately not yet to my knowledge been presented in English (not even that of the Second World War, in which Libyans cooperated at great cost with British against German and Italian forces). It is significant that a large part of this resistance traditionally came from Bedouin populations. Segre reports that, by the time the population of largely nomadic Cyrenaica was temporarily pacified in 1932, fully half of the population was in forced detention camps (*ibid.*, p. 151).

28 Ruth First, *Libya, the Elusive Revolution* (Penguin Books, 1974), p. 13.

29 Bianco, Mirella, *Gadafi, Voice from the Desert*, trans. Margaret Lyle (Paris, Editions Stock, 1975), p. 165.

30 Pamphlet, untitled, (Ottawa: Manshurat al-Zahf al-Akhdar, 1981, 4th edn., containing a sermon delivered on the occasion of the Feast of Sacrifice, 1980), pp. 20–6.

31 *al-Nadwah al-'Alamiyah* (Free University of Madrid), vol. 1, p. 297.

32 Qur'an 3:103.

33 Qur'an 30:30.

34 Qur'an 28:5.

Bibliography

Primary Sources

Arabic

al-Qadhdhafi, Mu'ammar, *Judhur al-Quwwah* (no publisher, place or date of publication; apparently a government publication).

———, *Khutab wa-Ahadith al-Qa'id al-Diniyah* (Tripoli, al-Quwwat al-Musallahah al-Libiyah – Idarat al-Tawjih al-Ma'nawi, n.d.).

———, *al-Kitab al-Akhdar* (*The Green Book*) (Tripoli, al-Markaz al-'Alami li-Dirasat wa-Abhath al-Kitab al-Akhdar, n.d.).

———, *al-Multaqa al-Fikri al-Awwal lil-Talabah al-'Arab al-Darisin bi-al-Jamahiriyah* (Tripoli, Manshurat al-Markaz al-'Alami wa-Abhath al-Kitab al-Akhdar, 1982).

———, *al-Sijill al-Qawmi*, 14 vols. – ____1969 – 1983 –____ (continuing annual publication, under various auspices).

———, *Shuruh al-Kitab al-Akhdar'* 2 vols. (Tripoli, al-Markaz al-'Alami li-Dirasat wa-Abhath al-Kitab al-Akhdar, 1983).

———, (pamphlet, untitled), 4th edn. (Ottawa, Manshurat Zahf al-Akhdar, 1980).

Western Languages

Ansell, Meredith O. and el-Aref, Ibrahim Massaud, *The Libyan Revolution: a Sourcebook of Legal and Historical Documents*, vol. 1, Sept. 1969 to Aug. 1970 (Wisconsin: Oleander Press, 1972).

Barrada, Hamid (with Marc Kravetz and Mark Whitaker), *Kadhafi: 'Je suis un opposant à l'échelon mondial'* (collection 'Les Grands Entretiens') (Paris, Editions Pierre-Marcel Favre, 1984).

Bleuchot, Hervé, *Chroniques et documents libyens, 1969–80*, Centre de Recherches et d'Etudes sur les Sociétés Méditerranéenes, Chroniques de l'Annuaire de l'Afrique du Nord (Paris, Editions du Centre National de la Recherche Scientifique, 1983).

Secondary Sources

Arabic

Husayn, Hasan Khalil, *al-Qadhdhafi wa-al-Thawrah al-Islamiyah* (Benghazi, Maktabat al-Andalus, 1973).

al-Jaza'iri, Muhammad ibn 'Abd al-Karim, *al-Qadhdhafi wa-al-Mutaqawwilun alayh* (Beirut, Dar 'Uqbah bin Nafi' lil-Nashr, 1982).

Salah al-Jibali, *Thawrat al-Fatih wa-al-Ishtirakiyah* (Tripoli, Maktabat al-Fikr, 1974).

al-Nadwah al-'Alamiyah Hawl al-Kitab al-Akhdar, 2 vols. (Qar Yūnus University, Benghazi, 1–3 Oct. 1972).

al-Nadwah al-'Alamiyah Hawl Fikr Mu'ammar al-Qadhdhafi – al-Kitab al-Akhdar (Free University of Madrid, 1–4 Dec. 1980).

al-Nadwah al-'Alamiyah Hawl Fikr Mu'ammar al-Qadhdhafi – al-Kitab al-Akhdar (Central University, Caracas, 1981).

Western Languages

Abdelsayed, Fr. Gabriel, 'Islam and State in Mediterranean Africa', *Africa Report*, March–April 1976, 42–5.

Anderson, Lisa S., 'Religion and Politics in Libya', *Journal of Arab Affairs*, 1, October 1981, 53–77.

Bianco, Mirella, *Gadafi, Voice from the Desert* (Paris: Editions Stock, 1975).

Cazalis, Anne-Marie, *Kadhafi, le templier d'Allah* (Paris: Gallimard, 1974).

Chambour, Raafat, *Pouvoir et Préceptes de la Révolution Libyenne* (Lausanne, Editions Méditerranéenes, 1977).

Chaarnay, Jean-Paul, 'Le Kadhafism', *Esprit*, 4, 1981, 42–51.

Cooley, John, *Libyan Sandstorm* (New York, Holt, Rinehart and Winston, 1982).

Damachi, U., 'Mo'ammar al-Gadhafi: Arab-Islamic Socialism in Libya', in U. Damachi (ed.), *Leadership Ideology in Africa: Attitudes toward Socio-Economic Development* (New York, Praeger, 1976).

Deeb, Marius K., 'Islam and Arab Nationalism in Al-Qaddafi's Ideology', *Journal of South Asian and Middle Eastern Studies*, 2, no. 2, Winter 1978, 12–26.

El-Fathaly, Omar I., and Palmer, Monte, *Political Development and Social Change in Libya* (Lexington, Mass. Lexington Books, 1969).

Finazzo, G., 'Islam e rivoluzione nella Repubblica Araba di Libia', *Studium* (Roma), 5, 1975, 663–96.

First, Ruth, *Libya, the Elusive Revolution* (Penguin Books, 1974).

Habiby, Raymond, 'Mu'amar Gadhafi's New Islamic Scientific Socialist Society', *Middle East Review*, Summer 1979, 33–9.

———, 'Qadhafi's Thoughts on True Democracy', *Middle East Review*, Summer 1976, 29–35.

Bibliography

Hjarpen, J., 'Mu'ammar al Kadhdhafi och Islam', *Religion och Bibel*, (Sweden) 35, 1976, 22–7.

Kooij, C., 'Islam in Qadhafi's Libya: Religion and Politics in a Developing Country', *Amsterdam Universiteit, Anthropologisch-Sociologisch Centrum*, Papers on European and Mediterranean Societies, 13 (University of Amsterdam, 1980).

Malvezzi, de' Medici, (Marchese) Aldobrandino, *L'Italia e l'Islam in Libia* (Milano, Fratelli, 1913).

Mayer, Ann, 'Developments in the Law of Marriage and Divorce in Libya since the 1969 Revolution', in *Journal of African Law*, 22, 1, Spring 1978, 30–49.

————, 'A Study of Islamifying Trends in Libyan Law since 1969', *Society of the Libyan Studies Annual Report*, 7, 1975–76, 53–5.

Robbe, Martin, 'Islam und Antiimperialismus (Bemerkungen zur islamischen Konponenten in der ideologischen Konzeption der libyschen Fuhrungskraften)' in *Libya – History, Experiences and Perspectives of a Revolution* (Asia, Africa, Latin America, Special Issue 8), (Berlin, Akademie-Verlag, 1980) 52–8.

Rondot, P., 'L'islam dans la politique des états du maghreb', *Politique Etrangère*, 38, 1973, 41–50.

Singh, K. R., 'North Africa', in *The Politics of Islamic Reassertion*, Mohammed Ayoob (ed.) (London: Croom Helm, 1981), 55–75.

Younger, S., 'Qaddafi: Faith and Freedom', *Middle East International*, 25, July 1973, 12–14.

Index

The Arabic definite prefix 'al-' is discounted in alphabetization.